Luther   _Jennifer_

ALL AMERICAN VEGAN
Veganism for the Rest of Us

Jennifer and Nathan Winograd

Photograph "Dewey Defeats Truman" reprinted with permission of the Wisconsin Historical Society at wisconsinhistory.org.

Hufu logo reprinted with permission of Argument from Design at ardes.com.

Photographs of Ronald Reagan and Ralph Nader reprinted with permission of Getty Images at gettyimages.com.

Photograph of Ithaca Journal reprinted with permission of Ithaca Journal at ithacajournal.com.

First Edition

Cover and original interior illustrations:
Kirk Waterman, watermancreations.com

All other interior illustrations:
iStockphoto.com

Cover design:
Judith Arisman, arismandesign.com

Interior design:
Almaden Books, almadenbooks.com

Library of Congress Control Number: 2011900332
ISBN: 9780979074332

Printed in China on recycled paper.

641.5636
WIN
05-19-2014

To our great-grandchildren.
May you inherit the world of which we only dream.

vegan

A vegan [vee-gun] diet is one free of all animal ingredients, including meat, fish, eggs, dairy, and honey. In other words, a vegan can eat any food not made from animals or containing animal ingredients.

ALL AMERICAN VEGAN

Family Owned and Operated Since 1995

A Love Story

Say the words "animal rights activist" to most people today, and they will conjure up an image of a person protesting, carrying signs, chanting slogans, or throwing paint. We've become a stereotype, and an angry one at that. But who are we really? And what are we so mad about?

Most people who describe themselves as "animal rights activists" also describe themselves as "animal lovers." For such people, becoming acquainted with the scope and magnitude of animal suffering and killing in our culture can be a shock. With most of it hidden from sight and cloaked in euphemisms, it is heartbreaking to become fully aware of how poorly humanity actually treats its fellow earthlings, killing billions of them every year for food, clothing, entertainment, vivisection, and even in our nation's animal "shelters." To love animals and suddenly find evidence of their abuse everywhere you turn—from what you eat to the shoes you wear, from the toothpaste you brush your teeth with to the pillow you lay your head on at night—makes it difficult to have faith in your fellow humans. The sheer magnitude of the abuse and killing is astonishing and just knowing about it can lead to feelings of helplessness, hopelessness and, not surprisingly, anger.

The resulting estrangement from our culture is often exacerbated by the lifestyle changes a respect for animals demands. Being an animal rights activist requires personal sacrifice, a reevaluation of daily choices most people take for granted. Adopting new values and changing what you eat, wear, and consider "entertainment" can strain your relationships with family, friends, and coworkers. And it can shape the way you view the world, yourself, and everyone in it.

Both of us began working in the animal rights movement over twenty years ago, and for many years thereafter we struggled with these emotions. While trying to make the world a better place for animals was gratifying, being immersed in jobs designed to combat animal abuse meant that we were also reminded of it constantly. We became bitter, believing that most people didn't care about animals or their suffering. Our indignation was fueled by the daily doses of bad news we received. After all, we worked at the very agencies people called whenever something bad happened to an animal.

Living in the trenches, we became myopic. We focused primarily on the bad things people did to animals, and we became blind to the good. Most regrettably, we lost the ability to perceive how most people really feel about

FOR THE ANIMALS: San Franciscan Jennifer Holdt (center) shouts at the driver of a truck towing a trailer full of livestock heading for the Petaluma Livestock Auction Yard on Monday morning

22-year-old Jennifer. She was mad as hell, and not going to take it anymore.

animals, and with that, an accurate sense of the animal rights movement's potential for success.

Then something happened that changed us, and has—as you will see—influenced the content of this cookbook. It started when we began to primarily devote our advocacy efforts to the No Kill movement, a field of animal rights that seeks to end the systematic killing of companion animals in our nation's pounds and humane societies. Through this work, we regularly encountered people who challenged our beliefs and perceptions. Over time these experiences eroded our prejudices and helped us see a more positive, hopeful, and, we now believe, accurate measure of humanity. Optimism replaced despair, not just about our fellow humans but about the great potential that *already exists* for building a more humane world for animals.

To explain exactly how this happened, we have to introduce this cookbook in a most unusual way: with a love story. It is not a story about a romance, a friendship between two people, or how one human feels about another. It is about how 100 million individuals of one species—humans—feel about 165 million individuals from others. But it is a love story nonetheless. And it begins in San Francisco over thirty years ago.

Lessons From the No Kill Movement

For most of its 140-year history, the Society for the Prevention of Cruelty to Animals (SPCA) in San Francisco killed tens of thousands of animals every year. By the late 1970s, over 20,000 dogs and cats were being im-

pounded annually, the vast majority of whom were put to death. Tragically, at that time, the San Francisco SPCA was typical of most "shelters" in the country in terms of both the appalling number of animals they killed and the excuses they offered for doing so. Leadership at the organization blamed the public, saying the problem stemmed from there being too many animals and not enough homes for them. They asserted that people were irresponsible—indeed, there was an epidemic of uncaring—which made killing the only option for most animals entering the "shelter." This mentality—and the brutal repercussions for the animals—defined the San Francisco SPCA throughout its history, until new leadership from outside the animal sheltering field took over in the late 1970s.

From the beginning, this new leadership was different. Optimistic and visionary, they did not believe that killing animals was inevitable. They also did not believe that the public was to blame for the killing. In total opposition to the conventional wisdom of the animal shelter industry and the animal protection movement, the new team believed that most people *did* care about dogs and cats and that if the SPCA harnessed their compassion, it could save rather than kill the animals entering the shelter.

And so they began to innovate, to develop new and revolutionary programs, many of them dependent on the goodwill and support of the citizens of San Francisco. These included comprehensive programs to maximize adoptions, provide alternatives to killing for unsocialized cats, offer low-cost neutering, and create volunteer opportunities. Members of the public walked

dogs, socialized cats, staffed offsite adoption venues, and cared for sick, injured, unweaned, and traumatized animals who needed extra TLC before they were ready for adoption. In short, the SPCA asked the people in the community, the very people their predecessors had blamed for the killing, to help save the lives of animals. And they did.

The results were nothing short of astounding. Cat deaths plummeted by over 70%, kitten deaths by over 80%, and dog deaths by over 65%. Of greater national significance, what the nation's largest animal protection organizations and virtually every "shelter" in the United States said was impossible—ending the killing of all healthy dogs and cats—became a reality for the fourth-largest city in the country's most populous state.

In the late 1990s, Nathan was working in a variety of leadership positions at the San Francisco SPCA, culminating in Director of Operations. Tragically, a new president began to dismantle the nuts-and-bolts programs that made No Kill possible. The organization abandoned its former goal of saving all the animals in San Francisco who could possibly be saved, including those suffering from treatable conditions. Having witnessed firsthand the incredible lifesaving made possible by simply changing the way a shelter operated, we believed in the model that the San Francisco SPCA had created. And we dedicated ourselves to proving that this innovative method held the key to ending the systematic killing of the millions of dogs, cats, and other animals entering our nation's pounds every year.

In order to do this, we wanted to disprove the many criticisms leveled against the San Francisco SPCA by those who felt threatened by its tremendous success, starting with the primary excuse they offered: lifesaving may have proved possible in an affluent urban area with a highly educated population such as San Francisco, but it could not be replicated in rural communities where, we were told, people are poor and have antiquated views of animals. We wanted to prove that what mattered was not where the shelter was located, but *who* was running it and how dedicated that person was to harnessing the public's compassion through programs and services, pioneered in San Francisco, that made a life-and-death difference for animals.

> What the nation's largest animal protection organizations and virtually every "shelter" in the United States said was impossible—ending the killing of all healthy dogs and cats entering a city's shelters—became a reality for the fourth largest city in the country's most populous state.

After fighting a losing battle to keep the San Francisco SPCA focused on its mission of saving lives, we moved to a rural community in upstate New York, where Nathan took over as the Executive Director of the Tompkins County SPCA, the animal control agency serving all ten towns and municipalities in the county.

Before we arrived, the SPCA in Tompkins County was typical of most shelters in the country: it had a poor public image; it killed a lot of animals; and it blamed the community for doing so. Once there, however, Nathan publicly announced his lifesaving goal and asked the community for help. Just as it was in San Francisco, the response was overwhelming. People from all walks of life volunteered, inspired by the goal. Many people adopted animals. Veterinarians offered their services at reduced rates or free of charge. Business owners offered free products as incentives to adopt. Nathan was not timid about asking for help, and most people were incredibly generous and eager to assist.

The goal of ending the killing of animals in the shelter became a community-wide effort. The people of Tompkins County opened their hearts, homes, and wallets like never before. And overnight, by harnessing that compassion and changing the way the shelter operated, Tompkins County, New York, became the first No Kill community in U.S. history, saving not only healthy animals but all treatable sick and injured animals as well. It didn't matter whether they were "cute and cuddly" or "old and ugly," blind, deaf, or missing limbs. They were all guaranteed a home, and they all found one.

The most amazing thing was that Nathan didn't have to convince anyone that this was a good idea or a worthy goal. The people of Tompkins County were ready and willing to make it a reality as soon as we got there. They just needed someone to tell them it was possible and to show them how to do it. And the achievement became a source of community pride, with bumper stickers throughout the county proclaiming "The Safest Community for Homeless Animals in the U.S."

We lived in Tompkins County for three years and then returned to California to start the No Kill Advocacy Center, a non-profit organization dedicated to spreading this new model of sheltering—what has since become known as the No Kill Equation—to shelters nationwide. And it *is* spreading, to every part of the country.* In some communities, shelter leadership has led the charge. In others, grassroots activists have forced the replacement of regressive leadership, hostile to their calls for reform, with new leaders who are passionate about No Kill and dedicated to making it a reality. But everywhere it is succeeding, it is succeeding because people in these communities have come forward to help. Why? Because Americans truly *love* dogs and cats.

As you might imagine, these positive experiences made us question our long-held assumption that we were in the minority regarding our concern for animals. We realized, thankfully, that we weren't so unique after all. And once the blinders were off, we saw evidence of the American public's love of dogs and cats everywhere we looked:

- The people who cross our paths on their morning dog walks;
- The stories, care, and embraces at our veterinarian's office (the waiting rooms never devoid of people, the faces of scared people wondering what is wrong with their animal companions, and the tears as they emerge from the exam room after saying good-bye for the last time);
- The bestselling books about animals that are written in ever increasing numbers because they touch people very deeply and very personally;
- The widespread popularity of movies about animals;
- The increase in specialty stores and services for animal companions;
- The steady increase in spending on our animals, even as other economic sectors may decline; and,
- The millions of dollars we give annually to humane societies and animal protection groups, making animal causes the fastest-growing segment in American philanthropy.

And the conclusion became inescapable: the animal protection movement had gotten it wrong. Our experience in Tompkins County proved that the story of the eight million animals entering "shelters" in this nation does not have to be a tragedy. Shelters *can* respond humanely and compassionately without resorting to killing. These shelters can be temporary way stations for animals, providing good care and plenty of comfort until they find loving homes. We also came to realize that the old excuse of rampant human uncaring and irresponsibility toward dogs and cats was simply not true. Because in order to make that case, one had to ignore the bigger, more optimistic picture of the 165 million animals in homes across the country cared for by people who go to great lengths to ensure their happiness and well-being. In short, we learned that there was enough love and compassion for animals in every community to overcome the irresponsibility of the few. And our hearts swelled.

But still we wondered: what about other animals? We were surrounded by the overwhelming evidence of people's love of dogs and cats, the animals many people regard as cherished family members, but how do they feel about animals with whom they do not have a personal relationship or bond? And an issue very dear to our hearts and why we have both been vegan for the last 20 years, *how do they feel about animals raised to be eaten?*

In our early animal rights days both of us would have scoffed at such a question. The question, we would have asserted, was an oxymoron given the fact that people were eating animals. "I like pigs" and "I like to eat pigs" are mutually exclusive propositions, are they not? We once thought so, but there are several reasons why the answer to that question is not so straight-forward for us anymore.

Unfortunately, how people *feel* about issues and what people *do* about them aren't always in sync, especially when aligning the two is inconvenient. Most Americans say they care about the environment, and maybe they do, but they are not riding their bicycles to work or driving electric cars. As a society we do not always make it easy to align beliefs with actions, and this cer-

---

*There are now No Kill communities all over the United States: in urban and rural areas, in the North and South, in the Western, Midwest, and Eastern parts of the country, and in both conservative and liberal states. It is also succeeding internationally too, as communities abroad embrace the No Kill Equation.

tainly could not be truer in food choices, as we discuss more fully in a subsequent chapter.

Second, there was the dramatic result of the November 4, 2008 election. Yes, we elected the first non-white President in our nation's history, but it was the passage of a proposition in California that made it historic for our purposes. That election not only answered the question, *how do people feel about animals raised to be eaten?* It also changed our understanding of what the animal rights movement can achieve on behalf of animals, how quickly we can effect change, and, perhaps most important of all, how we can most effectively do so at this time in history.

The Animal Movement's Own Bradley Effect*

Before 2008's historic election, even with candidate Barack Obama leading in the polls, Democrats secretly (and not so secretly) worried about what "white America" would do in the privacy of the polling booth. What they did is no longer a mystery.

New York Times columnist Frank Rich noted that "almost every assumption about America that was taken as a given by our political culture on [election] morning was proved wrong by [election] night." According to Rich,

> The most conspicuous clichés to fall, of course, were the twin suppositions that a decisive number of white Americans wouldn't vote for a black presidential candidate—and that they were lying to pollsters about their rampant racism. But the polls were accurate. There was no "Bradley Effect."

In California, an equally revealing vote on November 4, 2008 shattered another myth we hold about the public. The animal movement has been living with its own "Bradley Effect," the notion that Americans don't really care about animals. Thanks to Californians' response to Proposition 2, that notion has also been proven wrong.

Proposition 2 makes it illegal for animals (mostly chickens, pigs, and baby cows) on farms to be confined *"in a manner that prevents such animal from: (a) Lying down, standing up, and fully extending his or her limbs; and (b) Turning around freely."* It is a simple law but its reach is

extensive, affecting about 90% of chicken farms in the country's largest agricultural state.

Within the animal movement itself this legislation was somewhat controversial. Some said that such laws would actually harm rather than help animals by creating the illusion of "happy" eggs and meat, thereby making the choice to consume such products easier for people who might otherwise feel guilty about doing so. On the other side were activists who argued that it was unrealistic to place the bar so high—that so long as people eat eggs and meat, we should work to reform the most deplorable practices associated with their production so that we could lessen the animals' suffering.

It's an important debate, and one we address at the end of this book, but at the moment we want to share what this initiative—and its resulting success—taught us. In spite of internal debate about these issues within the animal movement, word of this controversy did not

---

*Wikipedia defines the "Bradley Effect" as "a theory proposed to explain observed discrepancies between voter opinion polls and election outcomes in some U.S. government elections where a white candidate and a non-white candidate run against each other... [T]he theory proposes that some voters tend to tell pollsters that they are undecided or likely to vote for a black candidate, and yet, on election day, vote for his white opponent. It was named after Los Angeles Mayor Tom Bradley, an African-American who lost the 1982 California governor's race despite being ahead in voter polls going into the elections."

state), and would increase the cost of eggs and other "groceries." They also argued that it would make "food" less safe.

In addition to industry groups, which spent nine million dollars in their campaign, most newspapers around the state also opposed the measure. The *San Francisco Chronicle*, one of the state's most liberal newspapers, urged readers to vote against Proposition 2, parroting industry arguments about its economic impact.

Moreover, political heavyweights in California and beyond came out in opposition, including the California Farm Bureau, California Small Business Association, and the Mexican American Political Association. Even the U.S. Department of Agriculture weighed in, spending taxpayer money on a campaign to defeat the legislation until a court ordered it to stop, finding that the agency's actions were an illegal use of its regulatory power.

And in an argument reeking of racism, some opponents went so far as to claim that ratification of Proposition 2 would result in an influx of cheap, unhealthy, and possibly tainted eggs from Mexico—an onslaught of "undesirable" egg immigration from South of the border.

reach the general public. After seeing photographs of hens crammed together into spaces the size of a desk drawer and being asked to outlaw the practice, the public widely regarded Proposition 2 as pro-animal legislation. Its level of support can therefore be considered as a good indication of where people come down on the issue of protecting animals in general—even animals they unfortunately regard as "food."

With polls showing that the economy and particularly loss of jobs was the foremost concern during that election on a wide range of issues, including the selection of our next President, and with the mainstream press arguing that Proposition 2 would result in loss of jobs and higher prices, conventional wisdom made the prospects for the initiative's approval appear grim. Why would voters risk these results in an economy already in a downward spiral to give animals a little more room on a factory farm?

In other words, Proposition 2 is a bellwether of just how enormous the political capital of animals has become. The vote to outlaw intensive confinement for pigs, chickens, and other animals had as its focus the protection of animals from some of the worst abuses of the factory-farming system. But the measure's resounding success at the polls had a far greater significance for *all* animals, because by all indications, Proposition 2 should have been defeated.

> Unfortunately, how people feel about issues and what people do about them aren't always in sync, especially when aligning the two is inconvenient.

But Proposition 2 passed. And it didn't *barely* pass. It passed by one of the widest margins of any proposition on the ballot, right up there with providing housing assistance to veterans. Roughly 80% of all counties in California approved the measure. It was nothing short of a landslide.

The opposition to Proposition 2, which outspent proponents by a three-to-one margin, argued that its passage would make California economically uncompetitive, would drive people out of business (or out of the

On the eve of November 4, 2008, we were unsure as to Proposition 2's prospects. The next day, we were dumbstruck by its resounding success. What we thought would be incredibly controversial turned out to be a "no-brainer" for most Californians. Regarding the idea of ending some of the most egregious cruelties of factory farming, the general public was well within its comfort zone. *How long had it been like this?* we wondered. *And what else might the animal rights movement accomplish?*

In fact, during the same election Massachusetts voters ended greyhound racing. In 2007 Oregon voters followed Florida's lead and banned gestation crates for pigs. And in 2006 Arizona voters passed a farm-animal protection statute banning veal crates, while Michigan voters defeated a measure to expand hunting. All of these victories proved the accuracy of polling which show that the vast majority of Americans think we should have strong laws to protect animals from abuse and that 96%—almost every single person—believe animals should receive some protection by law. Surveys also show that nine out of ten people believe we have a moral obligation to protect animals and over half have changed their lifestyle in some way to protect animals and the environment.

The conclusion to be drawn from these facts is that Americans don't just care about dogs and cats; they even care about animals with whom they do not have personal relationships. Most people are already concerned about animal welfare. Most people do not want animals to suffer. In short, despite those things that separate us as Americans, people from all walks of life want to build a better world for animals.

Of course, most Americans are not vegan. It is equally true that while Proposition 2 may have limited some of the cruelty, it did not abolish it or the killing, which makes an animal-based diet unacceptable. Although no ethical justification can *excuse* this complicity, we have struggled to understand the cause of this apparent contradiction, in order to grasp how we can most effectively overcome it, and thus bring peo-

ple's actions which affect animals more in line with how they actually feel about them.

After Proposition 2 passed we no longer regarded the overwhelming abundance of animal-based foods in our culture as clear evidence that people don't care about animals and that changing their minds, hearts, and diets would be a nearly impossible effort. If we were going to succeed, we had to approach the situation in a new way. But how? We found our answer one day when a series of serendipitous events made us suddenly able to read the writing on the wall, which in this case was actually scribbled on a backpack.

Lessons from a Tween Girl's Backpack

Like all seasoned vegans, we planned ahead when we took our kids to the amusement park. Having never been there, we weren't sure what vegan options to expect, so we packed a bag of food to take with us: sandwiches, cookies, and some fruit. But the best-laid plans...

At the entrance gate, we were informed that we couldn't bring in food and had to enter empty-handed. When we began to get hungry a few hours later, we scanned the menu boards of various snack bars. What we found was what you would expect at such a place: mostly pizza and fried food made from animals. After half an hour of searching for vegan options, we settled on a bag of potato chips and a banana for each of us, and walked to a nearby picnic table to eat our meager lunch. That's when we saw it and another piece of the puzzle fell into place.

On the ground next to our chairs was the

If everyone who ever tried being vegan succeeded, our numbers would increase dramatically. How can we make that happen?

A Recipe for Success

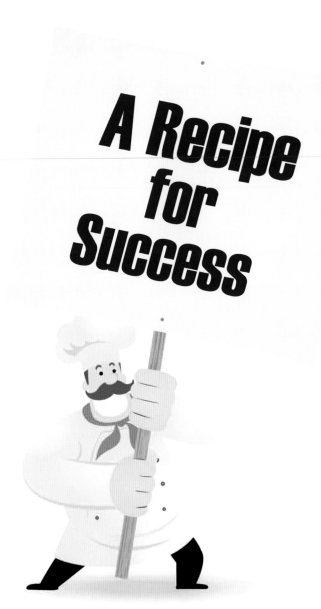

experienced one too many times situations analogous to our frustrating walk around the amusement park looking for something vegan to eat, and her determination apparently eroded. How many good intentions have gone awry because it wasn't as easy as it should have been for well-intentioned people to make ethical choices?

Every vegan can attest that there are three general responses when you first tell someone you are vegan. The first question concerns where you get your protein. The second is, "What about plants?"* The third, and most popular, is the confession that he or she once tried being vegan too but had to give it up for "health" reasons. This last response is paradoxical: read any book on the negative effects of an animal-based diet and you'll see it is akin to admitting that you had to start smoking again for your health. The fact that it is a common retort, however, actually bodes well for veganism. It shows how many people have made the calculation that being vegan would be a good idea. And it shows that people want to identify themselves with veganism. Being vegan is cool! But when confronted with someone who has succeeded, many people who have tried veganism and given up on it feel they need to offer a "defensible" reason or "political cover" for why they failed. For every vegetarian, there are three failed vegetarians. For vegans, the numbers who have fallen off the wagon is even more pronounced. The conclusion? We are a nation teeming with wanna-be vegans. So why aren't there more of us?

Of course, all the statistics regarding vegetarians and vegans are encouraging: our numbers *are* increasing every year. But if everyone who ever thought being vegan was a good idea, if everyone who ever tried being vegan actually succeeded, our numbers would increase dramatically. How can we make that happen?

A Recipe for Success

These days, it is totally feasible to be vegan—especially after you have taken the time to learn where to shop, what to shop for, how to substitute vegan for non-vegan ingredients when cooking, and when traveling or dining out, how to plan ahead. Mission: *totally* possible. But, truth be told, it is not always convenient. More than any other single factor, that simple fact accounts for why there are not more vegans. Nonetheless, the results of the No Kill movement, Proposition 2, and the

backpack belonging to a young girl seated near us, a backpack covered with writing and doodles intended to proclaim her burgeoning identity. Along with the scribbled names of bands and various celebrities, written in big, black letters was the word VEGAN, crossed out and replaced with the word VEGETARIAN. Here, no doubt, was a member of that blessed group that has always been the demographic most likely to embrace veganism—adolescent girls. Motivated by a love of animals, a growing appreciation of the larger world, and a desire for independence typical of her age, she had no doubt become aware of the suffering inherent in an animal-based diet and boldly proclaimed to her friends and family her intent to be vegan. And then, tragically, she

---

*Yes, what about plants? Because most crops are grown to feed animals raised for human consumption, following a vegan diet reduces the number of plants killed significantly. A vegan diet is therefore not only the most animal-friendly but also the most plant-friendly.

lessons from a tween girl's backpack suggest that the possibility of widespread veganism is great.

While in the past we would have written off the average person's professed concern for animals as disingenuous in light of the paradox "I love animals, but I also eat animals," we now recognize the importance of understanding what causes this unlikely juxtaposition, especially the roles played by inconvenience, custom, and how society has sanitized the brutal reality behind our "food" choices. For while most people's definition of what "loving" animals means may be radically different from that of most animal rights activists, there is much genuine concern for animals already there for us to take advantage of. And an accurate sense of the public's concern for animals is a barometer by which we should be measuring our potential for success and, at this time in history, how high we should be reaching on their behalf.

When asked about their vote in support of Proposition 2, most people claimed that they were unaware of the cruelties associated with factory farming. Once they were educated, most people were horrified to learn how animals are treated in these facilities and were eager and willing to bring such practices to an end. When the animal protection movement makes it easy for people to make choices that help animals, the public is likely to embrace them. Yes, some people may be uncaring, but most are concerned about animals and will support efforts to improve their lives. In short, make it easy for people to do the right thing, and they will.

Most people eat animals because they have always eaten animals. It is everywhere in our culture—in virtually every dish in every restaurant, in virtually every product in every supermarket, in virtually every recipe in every cookbook. Most people eat animals not because they have made a conscious decision to do so after having carefully weighed their options, but because they accepted it as necessary and inevitable long before they were old enough to give it much thought or prevent it from becoming an entrenched habit. According to evolutionary biologist Richard Dawkins, small children accept without question what adults in their lives tell them or model as appropriate behavior. It is a survival mechanism born of evolution.

Hence, in our culture, eating animals is just something you do. The practice is so ingrained that it is essentially invisible. Most people cannot conceive of what there is to eat if they don't consume animals and their products. And in most contexts, if they were to look around

Some people may be uncaring, but most people are concerned about animals and will support efforts to improve their lives. Make it easy for people to do the right thing, and they will.

for an answer beyond fruits and vegetables, other options wouldn't be immediately obvious. Thus the statement every vegan hears from incredulous relatives: *You must eat a lot of vegetables.* And when the answer is "no" (as is typical in the U.S. for both vegans and non-vegans), they follow-up with the inevitable question: *Just what do you eat then?*

And it is not just Great Aunt Inez in rural Illinois who is confused by the vegan diet. Even world-renowned chefs are. When the chef at San Francisco's Cliff House tries his hand at a vegetarian offering, he's lost, as the *San Francisco Chronicle's* restaurant critic discovered on a recent visit:

> The one dish that needs to be rethought is the vegetarian blue plate: a curried cauliflower custard that has the texture of pot de crème and an overwhelming roasted garlic flavor; a turmeric roasted half fennel bulb that needed brighter seasoning; and two roasted garnet yams... None of the flavors went together, and after a few bites my stomach flip-flopped and said stop.

Combine the fact that eating animals is deeply ingrained and pervasive in our culture, most people are removed from the sheer magnitude of suffering involved in the production of an animal-based diet and are rarely made to consider it, people are confused about how to eat vegan, and until recently there was a lack of appealing alternatives, and not only do you have an answer for the apparent contradiction, "I love animals but I eat animals," but you also have a solution.

We Hold These Truths To Be Self-Evident

Humans are capable of great change and great compassion. In just a few generations we ended monarchies and replaced them with democracies. In a short time historically, we went from the Pony Express to the Internet, and from a slave-based society to one that elected an African-American as our President. We outlawed child labor as well as segregation, we prohibited gender discrimination and are on the verge of granting marriage equality to all people regardless of sexual orientation. Once the path to a more compassionate future was cleared for them, most people who did not have a vested interest in the status quo pursued it willingly, because they saw it as better, and that kinder, more enlightened view became the new norm.

We spend a lot of time in the animal rights movement trying to convince people to philosophically embrace veganism and animal rights. It is often the backbone of our activism. That's because, ultimately, eating animals is wrong, and the harm caused by the practice is so great that that fact alone *should* be enough motivation for everyone to embrace a more ethical diet. But, unfortunately, while there are plenty of people who would agree with the message that harming animals is wrong, becoming vegan requires adjustments that many people find challenging in our culture, dominated as it is by animal-based foods. As a result, too many people who try being vegan fall off the wagon. We may win their hearts, but taking on their stomachs is a much more difficult proposition. The mind is willing, but the flesh is weak.

To win over aspiring vegans and vegetarians, we need to lessen the temptation to revert to old ways by making sure there is a tasty, readily-available vegan alternative to every meat, egg, and dairy-based food there is. We need to make vegan foods as accessible as non-vegan foods. In short, we need to promote and expand vegan convenience foods.

Doing so will foster positive change in significant ways. It will help aspiring vegans achieve veganism, which in turn will result in more converts. As anyone who has ever turned vegan and then watched his or her friends and family members follow suit knows, veganism is contagious. The animal rights movement grows as one vegan inspires others and converts them to the cause, and then these, in turn, do the same.

In addition, by creating a culture in which tasty vegan options are abundant, we can have a positive influence on the diets of people who have never considered going vegan. Over time such exposure will open minds and erode dietary prejudices. Ultimately, people won't miss or fight for what they don't feel they need, and our struggle to ensure animals' rights will be that much easier to accomplish. Quite simply, we can more effectively persuade people to become vegan if vegan food

Exposure bred familiarity, neutralizing suspicion of the unfamiliar and with it, resistance.

becomes as familiar, widespread, and appealing as the competition. That goal, as much as philosophically promoting the rights of animals, should be a primary objective of the animal rights movement.

It's all about exposure.

All Hail The Soy Latte

If you Google the words "soymilk" and "sales" together, you will be directed to many different articles discussing the tremendous growth of the soymilk industry over the last decade. Indeed, the sale of soymilk, and now other non-dairy milks such as those made from nuts, rice, and oats, is growing at an astounding rate. One website that tracks trends in the natural foods market notes that "Sales of refrigerated soymilk continue to accelerate, and industry experts see nothing that will impede the rapid growth."

Various suggestions have been offered as to why in the mid-1990s soymilk sales shot through the roof. Among them are greater environmental consciousness, increased diagnoses of lactose intolerance, the FDA's announcement that soy protein lowers cholesterol, and companies' shift to packaging soymilk in containers that required refrigeration in the dairy case, thereby increasing the product's visibility to consumers. Being longtime soymilk drinkers ourselves, however, we have an altogether different explanation for why 15 years ago we could find soymilk only at the local natural food store whereas now it is everywhere you look. One word: Starbucks.

When we first started living together a couple of decades ago, one of our favorite rituals was a walk downtown to a local café to enjoy what at that time was a rare vegan luxury—a latte made with soymilk. Big deal, you say? Ha! We lived in Marin County, the community just north of San Francisco, a place teeming with cafés, but one and only one offered soymilk.

Imagine, then, our surprise when we found another café that carried soymilk. On a trip to visit relatives in a small town in rural Illinois, where vegan food was so scarce we had to bring our meals packed in our suitcases, we nearly dropped dead from shock when we popped inside a brand-new Starbucks to get a mere cup of black coffee and left with sweet, steaming soy lattes. A similar experience occurred at another Starbucks just a few months later in Bakersfield, California, not exactly a vegan Mecca. But Starbucks are everywhere, which meant that soymilk suddenly was too.

Before Starbucks began carrying soymilk, only hippies, vegans, and Americans of Asian descent ever drank the stuff. And then a curious

> Quite simply, we can more effectively persuade people to be vegan if vegan food becomes as familiar, widespread, and appealing as the competition.

thing happened. Customers patiently waiting for the barista to prepare their drink overheard the person at the counter ordering a latte with soymilk. They glimpsed the frothy concoction handed over to the intrepid soul who ordered it and it piqued their curiosity. The next time they visited Starbucks, they tried soymilk and guess what? They loved it! And they told their friends, and so on and so on and so on.

Pretty soon it wasn't just Starbucks that offered soymilk but every other café as well, because the question "Do you have soymilk?" became ubiquitous. We now live in a nation where half of all people have tried soymilk. It is widely available at grocery stores and cafés throughout the country.

Why? Exposure bred familiarity, neutralizing suspicion of the unfamiliar and with it, resistance. As a result, Americans quickly and enthusiastically developed a taste for what had so recently been either unheard of or regarded as the most unappetizing of drinks—a milk-like liquid made from beans.

There is no end to the amazing things the animal rights movement could be doing right now to make it easier for people to make humane choices. The animal rights movement should be working directly with restaurants, supermarkets, and food companies to offer all-vegan analogs of the typical American diet. And that brings us to the philosophy that underlies this book.

All American Vegan

We wanted to create a cookbook that made veganism as easy as possible for the average American—one that met most people on their own terms by appealing to the modern American palate and by recognizing that most Americans today prepare their meals using prepackaged convenience foods. We wanted to make veganism familiar by simply veganizing the conventional American diet using vegan alternatives to the most popular American foods such as pizza, pancakes, hamburgers, and ice cream.

Ready-made vegan foods are coming of age. There are vegan products right now that were unthinkable just a few short years ago. There are, for example, vegan cheeses that look like dairy-based cheese, that melt like dairy-based cheese, and that taste like dairy-based cheese—without the cruelty, hormones, and saturated fats. And thank goodness. There is a strange dichotomy relating to food in contemporary American culture. People are more obsessed with cooking than ever before. Cooking shows are among the most popular on television; cooking websites are experiencing unparalleled traffic; food-related books top the bestseller lists. In fact, since 2002 sales of cookbooks in the U.S. have increased a whopping 30%. At the same time, ironically, the rate at which Americans cook from scratch is at an all-time low. Only 58% of people who cook at home on any given night do so from "scratch," as compared to 72% in the 1980s.

"Homemade dinners are dropping like a lead balloon," says an industry watcher who tracked the eating habits of 5,000 Americans over the course of a year. Cooking, it seems, has become recreational, something people do for fun—when the time to cook and the desire to do so coalesce—rather than a necessity. As a result, most people rely heavily on ready-made convenience foods when making dinner, so that even the definition of what constitutes "cooking" has changed. Making a meal by boiling water for pasta and heating jarred spaghetti sauce is now regarded as "cooking from scratch." And is it any wonder? It's a cliché but bears repeating: Americans lead busy, hectic lives. In many American families both parents work, and time for cooking is limited, so food that can be made quickly and conveniently is popular.

According to the U.S. Department of Agriculture, convenience foods now make up the bulk of the American diet, with the consumption of prepackaged foods increasing as much as 114% in some categories over the last two decades. Because that is how most Americans today eat, this cookbook is realistic and practical, introducing an abundance of ready-made vegan foods that imitate the meat, dairy, and egg-based staples of the American diet.

We also wanted to produce a cookbook that did not make veganism seem harder or less appealing than it actually is by confusing the "health" food movement with the movement to promote veganism. Too often veganism gets tangled up with "health" food, which in many cases means the introduction of unfamiliar dishes that alienate rather than excite aspiring vegans who have grown up on hamburgers and pizza. Because vegan foods by definition do not contain cholesterol and are generally lower in saturated fat, a balanced vegan diet is healthier than one based on meat, milk, and eggs. In fact, vegans have a reduced chance of developing lifestyle disease states, such as diabetes, heart disease, and cancer.

The health aspects of veganism are undeniable and a wonderful selling point. Nonetheless, to realize these benefits does not have to mean eating traditional "health" foods. In this cookbook we intentionally avoided telling aspiring vegans that they have to eat mostly vegetables, whole-grain bread, brown rice, or unfamiliar "healthy" foods like hemp kernels or adzuki beans. We wanted to appeal to Middle America, not just Beaujolais-sipping coastal liberals who would try exotic-sounding grains the Ancients used to eat even if we didn't tell them to. Quinoa? Spelt? Kamut? *No thanks*! But tell most Americans how to make a vegan Jello salad or "tuna" melt, and now you're talking!

> The health aspects of veganism are undeniable. Nonetheless, to realize these benefits does not have to mean eating traditional "health" foods.

To this end, our cookbook meets most Americans—you, the reader—where you already are. You love animals and are willing to embrace actions that spare them harm. You don't have three hours every night to cook. And you certainly do not believe that adopting cauliflower as a staple is a sustainable lifestyle change. We get it. Our goal is to make it easy for you to adopt a more humane diet. We don't want to replace your hamburgers with mung beans over a bed of alfalfa sprouts. We want to replace your hamburgers with hamburgers. To do that, we have veganized the American diet. The recipes will look familiar, will sound familiar, and for the most part will not require much preparation. Most importantly, they will be delicious. We believe that approaching dietary change this way will inspire you, and more people like you, to become vegan and thus help build a better world and a brighter future for our animal friends.

Happy humane eating!

The Art of Vegan Substitution

The eating habits of Americans are hot topics these days. With a move to regulate high-fructose corn syrup, partially hydrogenated oils, and sodium content as well as a growing obesity epidemic, there is no end to the "solutions" being offered to reform and improve how Americans eat. But not all solutions are created equal, and some are downright counterproductive.

Not long ago we watched a reality TV show in which a supposed "health" expert set out to reform the unhealthy habits of a typical American family. In addition to putting the family on a strict exercise regimen, she threw out the entire contents of their pantry and refrigerator. Out went the liters of soda. Out went the bags of potato chips. Out went the processed cheese spread, the cupcakes, and the lunch meats. Out went the take-out menus and "free delivery" flyers. She then gave the family a grocery list and sent them to the supermarket. As the mother entered the store's produce section, she turned to her children and said, "Kids, help me find the avocados. I think they're green, but I've never seen one."

Clearly here was a family with a diet in need of reform. But with a palate accustomed to traditional American fare—heavy on protein, salt, and sugar and light on plant-based foods—we wondered how the "expert" would set out to accomplish this formidable task. The answer was both tragic and hilarious.

Their first cooking lesson was a dish of tofu with shredded vegetables. And not just any tofu, mind you, but *silken* tofu. Now, silken tofu has its place. In vegan cooking, its silky texture and neutral flavor mean that it is often blended with other ingredients as a thickener or to make a dish creamier without imparting a strong flavor. But as for serving it as a main dish, especially to a family on red alert about so-called "healthy" food, it was not a wise choice. Because as useful as it may be, we must concede that silken tofu is not visually appealing. It's gelatinous and, quite frankly, looks a little slimy. If you fry it, it wiggles and jiggles and slowly falls to pieces. So as this dish of tofu and shredded vegetables was flipped repeatedly in the pan, the mixture began to clump together into a giant mass to which, inexplicably, no spices or flavorings were added.

Our increasing anxiety while watching the show was mirrored in the troubled eyes of the adolescent boy observing his mother cook the dish—a boy raised on hamburgers, hot dogs, and pizza who had cried when a bag of unopened chips was dumped into the trash. Scrutinizing the unfamiliar food his mother was preparing, he was no doubt conjuring in his mind the bleak and forbidding future of culinary deprivation that awaited him. When the dish was finally put before him and he was ordered to eat it despite his vehement protest, he took a bite, choked it down, gagged, and promptly regurgitated the food back out onto his plate.

Of course, it made for great television to watch a typical American kid choke down that much-maligned whipping boy of the health-food world—tofu. You couldn't help but laugh in spite of your pity. At the same time, we lamented what could have been. It was clear that the "expert" giving advice had not really done her homework. She equated healthy eating and vegetarianism with disgusting, unfamiliar food and Spartan deprivation. The alternatives that she offered were not only unpalatable, but also inedible, and therefore not helpful to the goal of teaching the family to make smart food choices in a way that would be sustainable. What a missed opportunity to educate not only the family, but the thousands of viewers about the amazing variety of vegan alternatives currently available to replace the worst health offenders in the American diet.

Had we been given the opportunity, we would have approached changing that family's eating habits in a very different way. We would have introduced them to the

wide array of vegan convenience foods now available that can replace the meat, eggs, and dairy products in their diet so that they could continue eating the foods they were accustomed to, but in healthier vegan versions. You can bet that we wouldn't have doomed that family with warmed-over unflavored tofu and vegetables. Instead, we would have fed them veggie burgers served on fluffy buns with grilled onions, ketchup, mustard, and pickles, or chickenless nuggets with a vegan Ranch dipping sauce, a pizza with veggie pepperoni, or even soy dogs with potato salad on the side. Would they have minded the changes? We seriously doubt it. And our cooking lessons would have included advice on how to use vegan substitutes for fat and cholesterol-laden animal products when following traditional recipes so that the change would be undetectable, which is how we have always approached cooking in our own home.

As any parent can tell you, kids are always hungry. Seldom does an hour go by when one of us doesn't hear the words, "I'm hungry," from either our son or daughter, if not both. With two hungry vegan mouths to feed in addition to our own, is it any wonder that an entire cabinet in our kitchen is filled with cookbooks? Dog-eared, soy sauce-stained, batter-encrusted cookbooks line our shelves, but one, more than any other, is our bible, the one we turn to time and again for inspiration and advice. Which is it? You'd never guess.

After forty years of combined veganism, the one we value most is a 1976 hand-me-down Betty Crocker cook book. No joke. If you can get past the 1970s-era photographs which somehow manage to make even cupcakes look unappetizing, and the meat-cut diagrams of animals' bodies which inspire in vegans the same horror as slave-ship schematics, the book offers a treasure trove of inspiration. All it takes is a little ingenuity to transform the 1,000 plus recipes into vegan ones. Knowing how to substitute vegan alternatives for animal-based ingredients; in other words, knowing how to veganize Betty Crocker (or Rachel Ray, Emeril Lagasse, or Martha Stewart) frees the American diet from its inherent animal cruelty, replaces unhealthy ingredients with healthier ones, and permits vegans to enjoy the foods we grew up eating.

> We believe that the easiest way to become vegan is to make the transition as familiar as possible—to "veganize" your favorite foods so that you can keep on eating them.

Making the Switch, American Style

We believe that the easiest way to become vegan is to make the transition as familiar as possible—to "veganize" your favorite foods so that you can keep on eating them. You are more likely to sustain the switch to a vegan diet over the long term if you don't have to give up the patterns of eating, cooking, and meal planning to which you have become accustomed. And today, more than ever, a vegan can eat what is by and large a conventional American diet, the menu you might find at your local diner, but in a totally animal-free way.

It's true! You can be vegan and still have pancakes for breakfast, a grilled cheese sandwich or a BLT for lunch, fried "chicken" with mashed potatoes and gravy for dinner, and chocolate cake with ice cream for dessert. Moreover, in spite of the great number of vegan cookbooks that want to introduce you to exotic grains you've never heard of with names you can't pronounce, eating unfamiliar highfalutin' sounding foods is not necessary in order to be vegan. So don't be discouraged. This cookbook will keep it simple and familiar. We will show you how to keep on eating like most Americans, minus the harm to animals, the planet, and yourself.

By the same token, if you enjoy whiling away your time in the bulk aisle of your local natural food co-op scooping quinoa, amaranth, and spelt into plastic bags, or if spending five hours a day preparing a dinner that will be eaten in 20 minutes is your idea of time well spent, put down this cookbook immediately, you have beans that need soaking. But if you agree with us and Ronald Reagan that ketchup is a vegetable and that cooking from scratch means opening cans and heating up the contents, then this is the vegan cookbook for you.

Get By With a Little Help From Your Prepackaged Friends

When we became vegan over two decades ago, the United States was just emerging from the Vegetarian Dark Ages. At that time, vegetarians (let alone vegans) were few and far between. Vegetarianism meant eating mostly bland hippie food—uninspired meals such as steamed vegetables over brown rice or lentil soup and whole-wheat chapattis. And trying to find a vegan option at a regular restaurant often ended in frustration and confusion for everyone involved. "You're a *what*?" the waiter would inevitably ask, leading to a drawn-out, tortured exchange which ended with our slowly spelling out the letters "V-E-G-A-N" to a bewildered waiter who thought we were insisting that we came from another planet.

Prepackaged vegetarian food was little better given the poor selection available at the dusty, funky-smelling vitamin store where we were forced to shop. Back then soymilk tasted like dirt, literally. Bread was so dense that you'd mistake it for a brick. And date-sweetened, whole-wheat carob cookies made you wonder time and again why you'd even bothered as you threw them half-eaten into the trash. The food was healthy, to be sure, and, it didn't harm animals, but eating it was no picnic.

Then, gloriously, the clouds began to part. Health concerns, improving ethics regarding animals, and the rise of the environmental movement have led to an evolution in vegetarianism. Now it's going mainstream, and it's going vegan too! In the last two decades the number of vegetarians has vastly increased. And with greater consumer demand has come more choices—more vegetarian restaurants and more natural food stores that surpass traditional supermarkets in terms of selection. According to a food-industry magazine, "Product innovation, media attention, and buyer demand are creating strong growth for the vegetarian foods market, and more companies are trying to profit from meat, egg, and dairy alternatives."

In fact, sales of ready-made vegetarian products are a billion-dollar industry in the U.S., and more Americans are eating soy-based meat substitutes than ever before. A trip to your local natural food store and, increasingly, the natural food section of your regular supermarket, is a tour de force of vegan options. Tasty vegan versions of meat (will that be fake "bacon," steak, or chicken?), cheeses (cheddar, American, Monterey Jack, mozzarella, or parmesan?), and ice creams (chocolate, vanilla, strawberry, or cookie dough?) abound. As do butter, egg, yogurt alternatives, non-dairy milks and creams of many varieties, and during the holidays, our family's favorite, nogs.

All these choices transform the question facing every new vegan, "What on earth do I eat now?" into "Which of these products do I choose?" and "What is the best way to incorporate them into my diet?" That is what this cookbook is all about. Taken as a whole the recipes in this book provide a primer in vegan cooking and baking. They are simple, familiar, and delicious recipes which will introduce you to a variety of vegan analogs and how best to use them. When combined with our One Week Menu Planner, they take the mystery out of sustaining the new vegan you.

A Typical Vegan Shopping List

Grains and Staples
Bread
Pasta
Cereal
Rice
Coffee
Tortillas
Frozen french fries
Frozen waffles
Instant mashed potatoes
Hamburger buns
Hot dog buns
Frozen pizza
"Chicken" noodle soup
All-purpose flour
Soup stock
Sugar
Rice and bean burritos
Pie crust
Peanut butter
Refried beans

"Meat"
Hamburger patties
Hot dogs
"Chicken" nuggets
Canadian "bacon"
"Turkey" slices
Ground "beef"
Stir-fry "chicken" strips
"Sausage" links
Seitan
Tofu

"Dairy"
Soymilk
Chocolate soymilk
Cream
Cheddar cheese
Mozzarella cheese
Yogurt
Sour cream
Cream cheese
Margarine
Egg replacer
Ice cream

Produce
Bananas
Apples
Watermelon
Mangos
Avocados
Strawberries
Pears
Grapes
Cherries
Blueberries
Lemons
Oranges
Spinach
Carrots
Onions
Potatoes
Lettuce
Celery
Tomatoes

Treats
Potato chips
Tortilla chips
Candy bars
Jelly beans
Soda
Donuts
Cake
Sprinkles
Chocolate frosting
Marshmallows
Ice cream cones
Apple pie
Fudge bars
Lollypops
Gummy bears
Cookies

Condiments
Mayonnaise
Instant "chicken" gravy
Instant "beef" gravy
Spaghetti sauce
Jelly
Soy sauce
Salsa
Hot sauce
Maple syrup
Ketchup
Mustard
Pickles
Relish
Guacamole

Same as it ever was, only better.

The Traditional Grocery Store

1 UNHEALTHY FOODS

2 UNHEALTHY FOODS

3 UNHEALTHY FOODS

HEALTH FOODS

HMMM

You can't say they didn't warn you.

Vegan Shopping

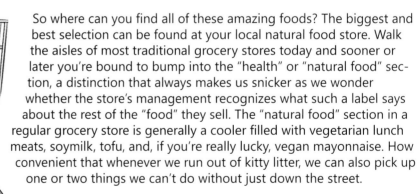

So where can you find all of these amazing foods? The biggest and best selection can be found at your local natural food store. Walk the aisles of most traditional grocery stores today and sooner or later you're bound to bump into the "health" or "natural food" section, a distinction that always makes us snicker as we wonder whether the store's management recognizes what such a label says about the rest of the "food" they sell. The "natural food" section in a regular grocery store is generally a cooler filled with vegetarian lunch meats, soymilk, tofu, and, if you're really lucky, vegan mayonnaise. How convenient that whenever we run out of kitty litter, we can also pick up one or two things we can't do without just down the street.

It's encouraging to see the ever-expanding selection of vegan foods in regular grocery stores, but if you're not doing most of your shopping at a store that specializes in natural foods, you're really missing out. The choices! The atmosphere! The time has come to make the switch. So grab a sweater *(why is Whole Foods always so damned cold?)*, drive that extra mile if needed *(bring your own bags to cancel any additional carbon emissions)*, find a cart *(don't forget to sanitize it with a free lavender-scented anti-bacterial wipe)*, and, if it's a co-op, check your fear at the door *(anyone can shop there, silly!)*.

From the welcoming aroma of freshly brewed coffee wafting from the in-store café, to the natural sunlight filtering through the skylights, from the hip, post-modern industrial architecture to the deli counter complete with corn-based biodegradable cutlery, traditional grocery stores simply cannot compete. No elevator music version of Ozzy Osbourne's "Crazy Train" *(of all things!)* mocking you from the speakers while you shop, but rather an obscure, forgotten, indie single you bought in the late eighties and haven't heard in years *(Hmm, what happened to that record? For that matter, what happened to all your records? Where did the time go? And is that wrinkled person in the mirror really you? WTF?)* And the staff? Alternative foods are a magnet for alternative lifestyles. Natural food stores are an eclectic mix of hippies, punks, Goths, Rastafarians, prairie skirts, tattoos, dreadlocks, Birkenstocks, Doc Martens, and body piercings. It's like a World Trade Organization protest, only they are smiling and helpful rather than smashing things and overturning police cars.

And then, of course, there's the food. It's different yet oddly familiar, like some healthier, alternate universe. You recognize the pictures on the boxes. Take the cereal, for example. Those are Cheerios, and those are Cocoa Pebbles, except that here they are organic and called something akin to "Wholesome O's" and "Endangered Coco Critters." And over there is an entire aisle of non-dairy milks of every variety—soy and rice and almond and coconut and hazelnut and oat and *oh my, does that really say hemp? Is that even legal?*

Where should you start? In the baking aisle where you'll find egg replacer, vegan cake mix, and vegan chocolate chips? In the dairy section with soy yogurt, vegan cream cheese, vegan sour cream, and margarine? In the freezer aisle featuring vegan pie crusts, vegan pizza, and non-dairy ice cream? Or there, among the vegetarian meats and cheeses, where vegan hot dogs, lunch meats, roasts, steaks, and fajitas sit patiently waiting alongside vegan cheddars, jacks, mozzarellas, and parmesans?

This world is your faux oyster!

REPLACING MEAT

Several years ago we discovered hickory seasoning, a liquid "smoke-in-a-bottle." Hickory seasoning imparts whatever you are cooking with a rich, smoky flavor eerily reminiscent of bacon. A bit too reminiscent for a vegan's comfort as the scent of it cooking fills your house with the unmistakable smell of cooking meat. The first time we used it to make the BLT recipe in this cookbook, both of us panicked that the vegan friends we were expecting might think we'd been cheating when they entered our house and inhaled.

We relate this story for the two valuable lessons it imparts. First, when using liquid smoke, proper ventilation is a must. And, second, it's not really the meat people crave but the added flavorings. Animal flesh in traditional cooking is a blank canvas until spices, flavorings, and other foods added to it turn it into sloppy joes, meatloaf, fried chicken, bacon, and hot dogs. Likewise, soy protein, tofu, and seitan—plant-based, protein-rich foods with chewy textures that mimic meat—are a vegan's tabula rasa. So bam! Get busy seasoning. Or if you're in a hurry, purchase the ready-made vegan alternatives to hamburger, steak, chicken, fish, and lunch meats now available and use them as you would if they were the animal-based product they are replacing.

IN PRAISE OF SEITAN

The one food that holds out the most promise for our animal friends at this time in history is seitan. Made from the gluten in wheat, seitan is our favorite food. It is chewy, readily absorbs flavors, and has a texture very similar to that of meat.

In our house we always have seitan on hand so that when dinner time rolls around, we have blank canvases for whatever we want as the centerpiece of our meal: fried "chicken," Buffalo wings, tuna melts, or Philly cheese steak sandwiches.

Making seitan requires a little time and effort, but a large batch whipped up at the beginning of the week should see you through until its end. But if you don't want to bother with making your own, many varieties of ready-made seitan are available at your local natural food store and will work just as well.

NO "BEEF" SEITAN LUNCH MEAT OR CUTLETS

TO PREPARE

Preheat oven to 300 degrees.

Grease a large mixing bowl with olive oil and wipe off excess.

Cutlets or Lunch Meat: In greased bowl, dissolve stock or bouillon in hot water, doubling the amount recommended by product label per cup. For example, if stock or bouillon requires 1 tsp. per 1 cup water to reconstitute, add 2 tsp. per cup instead. Since this recipe calls for 2 cups of water, you would therefore add 4 tsp. total. Do not use a pre-made liquid stock for this step, as it will not have enough flavor concentration.

Add soy sauce, browning sauce, and 1 Tbs. olive oil.

Separately, combine wheat gluten flour, soy flour, nutritional yeast, onion powder, and garlic powder.

Combine dry and wet ingredients, mixing for 2 minutes until the gluten is activated and the ingredients stick together to form a dough. If mixing by hand, grease hands with olive oil to prevent sticking.

Simmering Broth: In a large stockpot, bring all simmering broth ingredients to a boil and turn off heat. Pour simmering broth into a Dutch oven (unless stockpot is oven-safe).

For Cutlets: Slice dough into 10 even-sized pieces. Grease hands with olive oil and stretch each piece into a (roughly) 3 inch long x 4 inch wide x ½ inch thick cutlet.

For Lunch Meat: Slice dough into 2 even-sized pieces. Grease hands with olive oil and shape each piece into a (roughly) 6 inch long x 4 inch wide x 1½ inch thick loaf.

Sauté cutlets/loaves in olive oil until lightly browned, then place into simmering broth. It is okay if they overlap a bit.

Cover and bake 1 hour. Flip seitan pieces and cook for 1 hour more.

To make lunch meat, slice loaf as thin as possible immediately before using and sauté in oil and soy sauce. Store whole loaf and cutlets in broth.

Makes 2 lunch meat loaves or 10 cutlets

INGREDIENTS

- olive oil for greasing mixing bowl and sautéing cutlets

For Cutlets or Lunch Meat
- concentrated vegan "beef" or vegetable stock or bouillon (see preparation instructions for amount)
- 2 cups hot water
- ⅛ cup vegan soy sauce
- 1 tsp. browning sauce*
- 1 Tbs. olive oil
- 3 cups wheat gluten flour
- ¾ cup soy flour
- ⅓ cup nutritional yeast
- 1 tsp. onion powder
- 1 tsp. garlic powder

For Simmering Broth
- 8 cups hot vegan "beef" or vegetable broth (either premade or reconstituted according to package directions)
- 1 cup sliced mushrooms
- ½ cup diced onions
- 1 tsp. browning sauce
- 3 inch x 1 inch piece of ginger root, peeled
- 3 inch x 4 inch piece of dried kombu**

---

*Browning sauce is a blend of caramel color, vegetable concentrates, and seasonings. It is used to add a dark color to foods which is helpful when making vegan "beef" as seitan is naturally light in color. Look for it in traditional grocery stores.

**Kombu is a type of seaweed. Look for it in the Japanese section of natural food stores.

NOT "BACON" STRIPS

Serves 4

INGREDIENTS

- 2 Tbs. nutritional yeast
- 3 Tbs. soy sauce
- 1 Tbs. liquid smoke hickory seasoning
- 1 Tbs. maple syrup
- 4 Tbs. canola oil, divided
- ½ pound firm tofu, pressed and sliced into 4 inch long x 1 inch wide x ¼ inch thick strips (see p. 35 for directions on how to press tofu)

TO PREPARE

In a large bowl, combine nutritional yeast, soy sauce, hickory seasoning, maple syrup, and 3 Tbs. canola oil.

Add tofu strips and stir to coat. Marinate for at least 1 hour, stirring occasionally.

Heat remaining 1 Tbs. of oil in pan over medium heat and add drained tofu strips.

Cook until crispy, 3-4 minutes, then flip and crisp other side as well, adding more oil as needed to prevent sticking and burning.

Serve as a breakfast side dish or in a BLT (recipe, p. 84).

NO TUNA FISH SALAD

Serves 4

INGREDIENTS

- ½ cup vegan mayonnaise
- 1 tsp. yellow mustard
- 1 tsp. kelp granules
- ½ tsp. black pepper
- ⅛ tsp. salt
- 1 Tbs. capers, drained
- 1 Tbs. vegan sweet relish
- ⅛ cup diced red onion
- ⅛ cup diced celery
- 8 oz. (1 package) store-bought shredded seitan or 1 cup shredded homemade no chicken seitan cutlets (recipe, p. 34)

TO PREPARE

In a large bowl, combine all ingredients except seitan.

Add seitan and stir to combine.

Serve in a sandwich (recipe, p. 89). For a tuna melt, follow the recipe for grilled cheese sandwich (recipe, p. 87), adding several Tbs. of no tuna fish salad.

NO CHICKEN SEITAN LUNCH MEAT AND CUTLETS

Makes 2 lunch meat loaves or 10 cutlets

INGREDIENTS

- olive oil for greasing mixing bowl

For Cutlets or Lunch Meat
- concentrated vegan chicken stock or bouillon (see preparation instructions for amount)
- 2 cups hot water
- 4 Tbs. cashew cream (recipe, p. 39)
- 2½ cups wheat gluten flour
- ¼ cup soy flour
- ⅛ cup oat flour
- ¼ cup nutritional yeast

For Simmering Broth
- 8 cups hot vegan chicken broth (either premade or reconstituted according to package directions)
- 1 cup cashew cream
- 1 cup sliced mushrooms
- 1 tsp. minced garlic
- ½ tsp. onion powder
- ⅛ tsp. celery seed
- 1 bay leaf
- 1 Tbs. olive oil

TO PREPARE

Preheat oven to 300 degrees.

Grease a large mixing bowl with olive oil and wipe off excess.

Cutlets or Lunch Meat: In greased bowl, dissolve stock or bouillon in hot water, doubling the amount recommended by product label per cup. For example, if stock or bouillon requires 1 tsp. per 1 cup water to reconstitute, add 2 tsp. per cup instead. Since this recipe calls for 2 cups of water, you would therefore add 4 tsp. total. Do not use a premade liquid stock for this step, as it will not have enough flavor concentration.

Add cashew cream and stir to combine.

Separately, combine wheat gluten flour, soy flour, oat flour, and nutritional yeast.

Combine dry and wet ingredients, mixing for 2 minutes until the gluten is activated and the ingredients stick together to form a dough. If mixing by hand, grease hands with olive oil to prevent sticking.

Simmering Broth: In a large stockpot, bring all simmering broth ingredients to a boil and turn off heat. Pour simmering broth into a Dutch oven (unless stockpot is oven-safe).

For Cutlets: Slice dough into 10 even-sized pieces. Grease hands with olive oil and stretch each piece into a (roughly) 3 inch long x 4 inch wide x ½ inch thick cutlet.

For Lunch Meat: Slice dough into 2 even-sized pieces. Grease hands with olive oil and shape each piece into a (roughly) 6 inch long x 4 inch wide x 1½ inch thick loaf.

Place cutlets/loaves into simmering broth. It is okay if they overlap a bit.

Cover and bake 1 hour. Flip seitan pieces and cook for 1 hour more.

To make lunch meat, slice loaf as thin as possible immediately before using and sauté in oil and soy sauce. Store whole loaf and cutlets in broth.

Vindicating Tofu

When it comes to a bad reputation, tofu is right up there with New Jersey and mothers-in-law. But it shouldn't be. No law says that vegans *have* to eat tofu, but the truth is that, if you don't, you're missing out.

Tofu is truly a wonder food. Made from soybeans and rather bland-tasting by itself, tofu easily absorbs the flavors of the sauces or marinades in which it is soaked, especially if it is pressed first. Available in different textures from extra firm to silken, it is endlessly versatile. Freeze tofu, and it becomes chewy—perfect for a ground-beef substitute in sloppy joes. Mix firm tofu in a blender with lemon juice, garlic, and a little salt, and you have a ricotta substitute for lasagna. And silken tofu is great for making vegan desserts such as puddings and pies. So, please, give tofu a try. Chances are you won't regret it.

The Tofu Pressing Enterprise

If you are using a recipe which calls for pressed tofu, you may be able to find tofu that does not need pressing, and will be labeled accordingly. If you cannot find "extra-firm," "pre-pressed," or "reduced-moisture" tofu, buy the firmest tofu you can find and press it yourself. You can find tofu presses for sale online or you can also press tofu the Rube Goldberg method using plates and books.

After you remove the tofu from its package, drain off the liquid and pat it dry. Line a dinner plate with napkins or paper towels and place the tofu on top. Place another dinner plate on top of the tofu so it resembles a sandwich, with a tofu center and the plates acting as the bread slices facing one another. Then stack heavy books on the plate. Finally a practical use for those Norton anthologies of English Literature you've lugged around since college. How many are needed? Most likely two. While the crushing weight of The Canterbury Tales (Volume I) may be enough to get your tofu misty, to really make it weep may require the Romantics (Volume II). But don't overdo it or the tofu will break apart. Pressing tofu is one of those cases where *more* is not always better. Add that volume of American literature, with its heady words extolling liberty and independence, and your tofu may rebel, fracturing and bringing the whole damn empire, 'er enterprise, crashing down.

During pressing, which takes about 40 minutes, you'll need to periodically drain away the liquid that has accumulated on the plate. Do so, replace the napkins or paper towels, and then reassemble until the tofu is drained of liquid, and ready for whatever magical transformation you have in mind.

It Doesn't Have to be This Whey!

Replacing Dairy Products

It has been said of vegans that we practice our diet with the fervor of religious conviction. And, as in any religion, we have our rituals. One of our most important observances, of equal significance to the "Grilling of the Waiter" sacrament, is the one we ceremoniously perform whenever we encounter a new or unfamiliar product at the grocery store—the "Reading of the Label." We need to know: vegan or heretic? No ordinary experience, the "Reading of the Label" has all the gravity of a search for hanging chads: sweat pours off your brow, eyes bulge wide, and the mouth appears slightly agape, ready for the cheer or grunt that invariably follows.

At its core, this practice is one of faith in natural food companies. We take the time to interrupt our shopping with an ingredient-by-ingredient scan of a product fairly confident that in this day and age any new vegetarian food will be suitable for the booming number of vegans as well. Sometimes, however, our trust is betrayed, and these are the times that try our souls. How many vegans can relate a similarly tragic tale: from across the aisle they catch your eye—a new type of cookie. Perhaps they'll taste like Chips Ahoy, your childhood favorite! Admonishing yourself to curb your enthusiasm until you can confirm the product's veganocity, you approach the colorful display and pick up the box of cookies to read the ingredients. Halfway through your scan of the so-far totally vegan list, you begin to convince yourself that everything is going to work out fine, when suddenly... No way! Does that say *whey*?* "Dang," you mutter to yourself as you dejectedly put the cookies back on the shelf.

It doesn't have to be this way! That one party-crashing ingredient defiling an otherwise totally vegan product simply isn't necessary. It can easily be replaced with a vegan alternative. Here's an amazing yet little-known fact to most non-vegans: eggs, butter, milk, and their various derivatives are not required when baking cookies, cakes, pies, or pastries. These animal products can be substituted with a vegan alternative with no substantive change to the taste or texture of the treats. Yet many companies marketing vegetarian products continue to lose the vegan market share. While we wait for them to figure this out and adjust their products accordingly, we'll content ourselves with buying the many vegan treats already available or with veganizing old favorites in our own kitchens.

Vegan or not vegan? That is the question. A photograph made famous during the presidential election of 2000. The hanging chad has taken on mythic proportions. In reality, this vegan vote-counter is surveying a lunch menu's list of ingredients.

---

*Whey is a dairy product, the liquid that remains after milk has been curdled and strained to make cheese.

Replacing Butter

Fats are important when cooking and baking because they give a product richness, flavor, and tenderness or crispiness. Fortunately, butter and shortening can be easily replaced with vegan margarine or vegan shortening. Most vegan margarines and shortenings no longer contain artery-clogging partially hydrogenated oils. But beware: not all margarines and shortenings are vegan. Many contain animal fat, whey, casein (a milk derivative), or butter flavoring, so be sure to read labels.

Replacing Milk & Cream

There was a time, and not so very long ago, when veganism was a lot less creamy than it is today. Sure, we had soymilk and rice milk, and ice cream made from both. But there was no cream cheese, no sour cream, no yogurt, no cream (whipped or otherwise). And except for this strange rubbery stuff in a tube, no cheese either. How times have changed! All of these foods now come in a wide variety of non-dairy versions. Some are made from soymilk, some from rice, and others from nuts and coconuts. Whichever you prefer, use them as you would the originals when cooking and baking, bearing in mind the following points.

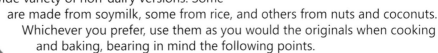

As ingredients milk and cream serve several purposes: flavor, moisture, texture, and, when baking, a softer crumb. Non-dairy substitutes can easily replace milk, but when choosing which one, be sure to take into consideration the flavor and density of what you are substituting. Most brands of non-dairy milk come in a variety of flavors: usually plain or regular (sweetened and unsweetened), vanilla and chocolate. When replacing milk in a sweet recipe, you can use the regular or vanilla, sweetened flavors. If you are replacing milk or cream in a savory recipe, such as a soup or mashed potatoes, use only the plain or unsweetened variety. Also, if you are replacing whole milk, you will want to use thicker non-dairy milk, such as regular soymilk, and not the lower-fat varieties, which are thinner. If you are substituting cream in a recipe, be sure to use a vegan non-dairy cream/creamer. But beware: the non-dairy creamers intended for coffee sold in traditional supermarkets are often not vegan and may contain flavorings that could ruin a recipe.

What is the Value of a Life?
The Skeletons in Jennifer's Closet

I used to work in a specialty cheese shop. I was surrounded by cheeses from around the world and I knew the unique history and characteristics of each of them. Blindfolded, I could tell the difference by smell and taste. At the tender age of 20, I was a gourmet, a bona fide connoisseur of artisan cheeses. Every day, I lived, breathed, ate, and according to my roommate, smelled like cheese. I was proud of that at one time. Even after becoming vegan, I pined for cheese. At least, I used to until I met someone who made me lose my craving forever.

"Drop calf" is the industry term for baby cows who are taken from their mothers to be sold for slaughter. To a dairy farmer, a baby cow is competition for his mother's milk and therefore an unnecessary cost. Along with animals the industry considers "old" or "worn out" because their production has slacked, "drop calves" are sold to the highest bidder at stockyard auctions throughout the country. These are the animals who end up in pet food or in cheap, frozen TV dinners. They also have their stomachs scraped after being killed for rennet, an ingredient in cheese.

As part of my work with an animal rights organization, I visited auctions to document what I saw. And what I saw was heartbreaking. But one particular image still haunts me: a tiny newborn calf covered in amniotic fluid, lying all alone in the corner of a dirty pen one bitter cold morning. Barely a few hours old, he looked bewildered, fearful, and in desperate need of his mother. "If he survives," said a worker when I asked about him, "he'll probably sell for a dollar or less." *One dollar.* That is what his life was worth to the dairy industry.

Since that moment, the thought of eating cheese or anything made from milk literally turns my stomach. Because now, whenever I see such foods, I see him too. I see his disoriented expression. I see him shivering alone in a dirty pen. I see him cowering in the corner, wet with amniotic fluid. I see him again and again and again whenever someone asks about my veganism and then tells me they could never give up cheese and other dairy products. "I love it too much" they might say, searching my expression for some hint of agreement. Instead, I think of the baby cows that milk really belongs to, the milk that is their birthright, and upon which their very lives depend. And I see it cruelly taken away because the person standing before me likes the fleeting taste of pizza, ice cream, or a glob of camembert spread upon a water cracker. And I think: is that what their lives are worth?

Got milk? Never again.

How to Make Cashew Cream

Cashew cream is often a wonderful replacement for dairy cream. Cashews have a neutral flavor but are high in fat. When soaked and liquified in water, they make a perfect alternative in some dishes that calls for cream, such as mashed potatoes, cream-based soups, and desserts. Cashew cream is simple to make. Here's how to prepare it:

Cover raw, whole cashews with water in a large pot and bring to a boil. Immediately turn off heat and soak for one hour. You can also soak the nuts for at least 12 hours instead of cooking them. Soaking rather than boiling the cashews helps them retain their natural sweetness.

Strain off the water and place the cashews in a blender.

Cover cashews with fresh water to 1½ inches above the top of the cashews.

In a blender, process until silky smooth, with no chunks (however tiny) remaining.

Store cashew cream in refrigerator. Shake well before using. Because it tends to thicken over time, when using cashew cream in a recipe, consider the consistency of the dairy product you are replacing. If necessary, add water to thin it out.

Some Helpful Vegan Baking Tips

Baking times are only estimates, as many factors including the peculiarities of your oven and bakeware can affect how long an item takes to bake. Changes in ingredients can also affect baking time. Be sure to follow directions regarding how to test for doneness. And consider that, when using soymilk, color is not always a good indicator. Soymilk can sometimes cause a product to brown before it is done, especially along the edges. If this begins to occur while baking, cover the baked good loosely with aluminum foil. This will help to slow edge browning by directing the heat back to the center and away from the outside. Sometimes adjusting the rack position in your oven helps too.

All Roads Lead to...

Give me a break!

Breaking the Habit

This cookbook includes vegan recipes for some of the most popular American dishes in which eggs are the main ingredient, such as omelets, scrambled eggs, and egg salad. In most recipes using eggs, however, they are not the centerpiece but are included to serve a particular purpose that can be replaced with a vegan alternative. The next page lists a variety of vegan options to use instead of eggs.

Instead of Eggs

In baking, eggs generally serve two purposes—as a binder for the ingredients or as leavening, which helps the item you are preparing rise. Substitutes for each egg being replaced include:

• Powdered egg replacer that is sold in the baking aisle of natural food stores. This can be used when the recipe calls for egg whites or egg yolks as well. It works in both sweet and savory recipes. Powdered egg replacer requires that it be blended with water at a specific ratio prior to use. When the recipes in this cookbook call for egg replacer powder, it should be in the reconstituted form, following package directions, unless the recipe does not tell you to do so.

• Vigorously mix 1 Tbs. ground flax seed (ground in coffee or spice grinder) and 3 Tbs. warm water

• ¼ cup blended silken tofu

• ½ banana blended until smooth (use only if a slight banana flavor is acceptable in the recipe)

• ¼ cup applesauce (use only if a slight apple flavor is acceptable in the recipe)

• ¼ cup vegan mayonnaise (use this alternative only when the recipe also calls for baking powder)

• ¼ cup vegan plain soy yogurt (use this alternative only when the recipe also calls for baking powder)

• Blend 2 tsp. baking powder, 1 Tbs. vegetable oil, and 2 Tbs. warm water

• Separately add 2 tsp. baking powder, 1 Tbs. apple-cider vinegar, and 1 Tbs. warm water to the batter

THIS DOTTED RED LINE REPRESENTS THE MAXIMUM AMOUNT OF SPACE ALLOTTED TO 97% OF CHICKENS RAISED FOR EGGS IN THE UNITED STATES. 15% OF THOSE CHICKENS HAVE EVEN LESS ROOM THAN THIS.

3% OF ALL EGG-LAYING HENS ARE LABELED "CAGE-FREE" OR "FREE-RANGE." WHILE THEY ARE NOT IN CAGES, THEY ARE OFTEN CRAMMED TIGHTLY TOGETHER IN LARGE WAREHOUSES, WITH ONLY A FEW MORE INCHES OF SPACE THAN CAGED CHICKENS, AS REPRESENTED BY THE DOTTED GREEN LINE. CONTRARY TO WHAT THE LABELS IMPLY, THE VAST MAJORITY DO NOT HAVE OUTDOOR ACCESS.

NUTRITIONAL YEAST
A Rose by Any Other Name Would Smell as Sweet

In the 1950s, American importers trying to create a market for the New Zealand fruit we now call "kiwi" had a problem. They were called "Chinese gooseberries" when red China was seen as a communist menace, and talking heads predicted that the Korean War would inevitably lead to war with China. Eating Chinese gooseberries was considered downright un-American. It didn't help that in spite of the fact that kiwis are sweet, delicious, and a pleasing lime green color on the inside, they are brown and hairy on the outside. In other words, they looked and sounded like something that came out of, rather than something that should go into, your body, if you catch our meaning. Then American importers hit on what is considered one of the best marketing strategies in history. They changed the name to "kiwifruit" and sales soared.

In the vegan world, we have our own Chinese gooseberry, our own awful sounding but delicious tasting food—*nutritional yeast*. Technically speaking, nutritional yeast is a deactivated yeast, grown in a mixture of sugarcane and beet molasses then washed and dried out. It comes in yellow flakes or as a powder that looks like fine cornmeal and can be found in the bulk aisle of natural food markets.

Why are vegans so crazy about the stuff? Because it tastes like cheese. And what's more, it is low in fat and sodium, and as the name proclaims, nutritious—high in protein and B-complex vitamins. Yet in spite of its many wonderful attributes, nutritional yeast is relatively unknown outside the natural food world. We blame its awful name. Honestly, could it get any worse? But don't let the label fool you. Until there is a tiny bottle of vegan flavoring marked "cheese" in the spice section of our grocery stores, right next to the vanilla, coconut, and lemon extracts, nutritional yeast is essential to a well-stocked vegan kitchen. Someday, hopefully soon, a marketing genius will rebrand one of our best kept secrets with a name more befitting its qualities, and this tasty powdered gold will finally hit the big time.

Don't Hold the Mayo!

No vegan cookbook, especially this one, would be complete without mentioning vegan mayonnaise, since the traditional American diet is replete with the stuff. Thankfully, delicious ready-made vegan mayonnaise is now widely available. See our website for product recommendations.

Busy as a Bee

The old cliché "busy as a bee" couldn't be truer. Bees spend all day flying from flower to hive and from hive to flower and back again, over and over, day in and day out. Those who don't leave the hive spend their days in endless toil, caring for baby bees, fanning nectar, and serving the queen. No vacations, no coffee breaks, no retirement. And after all of this hard work, which in the process pollinates our food supply and blesses us with flowers, what is their reward? The rich honey they worked so tirelessly to produce? Nope. Humans knock them out by pumping smoke into their hives, then steal their honey to sell, replacing it with a less nutritionally complete sugar substitute. And that's not all. Bees must fly thousands of miles to yield just one pound of beeswax. That's enough to make only one beeswax pillar, a heck of a lot of work just to have humans send it all up in smoke. Give bees a break! Use soy candles and sweeten that tea with vegan sugar, agave, or maple syrup instead.

TOOLS OF THE TRADE

There is nothing about the process of vegan cooking and baking that is all that different than cooking and baking traditionally. To whip up a delicious vegan cake, for example, requires the same kitchen utensils and appliances as making one that contains animal ingredients. However, there are three tools that make the preparation quicker, easier, and even more fun. They are the holy trinity of the well-tooled kitchen: the stand mixer, the food processor, and the blender.

What's for breakfast, lunch, and dinner?

VEGAN
MENU PLANNING

The traditional American diet generally builds a meal around a protein. Unfortunately, that protein is usually animal-based, but you can approach meal-planning as a vegan in the same way. Once you decide what the centerpiece of your meal will be, consider foods that will complement your choice. For example, a popular American meal is fried chicken. Often it is served with mashed potatoes, biscuits, and gravy. This, like many other typical American "foods," can be enjoyed in a vegan version as well. So by all means, do so.

When meal planning, keep it familiar. Eat the foods you already eat but in vegan versions. Use your favorite traditional cookbooks but employ substitutions. Satisfy those cravings but veganize them first. Before you know it, being vegan will be as familiar and simple as the way you eat now.

Dining Out While Vegan

While this cookbook is intended to assist you in preparing all of your favorite American foods at home, we also want to provide tips on dining out as a vegan. If you live in Los Angeles or New York City, you are in for some of the tastiest vegan fare on the planet. In other locales, however, it can be a challenge which will hardly serve you as a new vegan. Except, of course, if you plan ahead! Visit allamericanvegan.com for vegan options at chain restaurants, links to veg-friendly eateries, and safe bets when eating at Chinese, Indian, Japanese, Mexican, and other ethnic restaurants.

IT'S ALSO ABOUT YOU!

There are many altruistic reasons to become vegan: the welfare of animals, the health of our planet, and even the well-being of our fellow human beings. But don't forget self-interest: being vegan is good for you too! You don't need meat, eggs, or dairy products. You never did, and you never will. So stop worrying that a vegan diet means analyzing everything you eat. A vegan diet will give you the nutrition you need not just to survive, but to thrive.

Not All Soymilks Are Created Equal

When familiarizing yourself with new foods, remember to experiment. Not all soymilks, seitans, tofus, and vegan cheeses are created equal. Just as most people have their favorite brands of traditional foods, the same is true of natural food brands, and what appeals to one person might not necessarily appeal to you. Take a poll of a dozen vegans and ask them what their favorite non-dairy milk is, and we guarantee that you'll get a dozen different answers. Want proof? Look in our cart when we go shopping. There is vanilla sweetened almond milk for Jennifer, vanilla soymilk for Nathan, and vanilla coconut milk for Riley. For Willoughby, who suffers from a soy allergy and prefers vanilla soymilk like his dad, there is both vanilla and chocolate rice milk. Yes, we have a very crowded refrigerator.

"Experiment.
Make it your motto, day and night.
Experiment, and it will lead you to the light.
If this advice, you always employ,
the future will offer you infinite joy and merriment.
Experiment, and you'll see."

–Cole Porter

The texture and flavor of foods vary tremendously from brand to brand, so don't give up and assume you don't like soymilk (or seitan or vegan cheese) because you tried one variety and were underwhelmed. Try another. Moreover, new products are coming out all the time. Keep your eyes open when shopping for the newest brand of veggie dog, veggie burger, or vegan cheese to try. And keep checking our website at allamericanvegan.com for reviews of new products.

Also, if your local grocery or natural food store doesn't carry an item mentioned on our website, ask them to order it. The brands we recommend tend to be from large companies with national distribution, so your local natural food store or even your regular supermarket should be able to acquire them.

Hocus Pocus, It's Vegan!

*Veganize
Spaghetti with Meat
Sauce and Garlic Bread*
Almost all dry pasta, unless it is labeled an "egg noodle," is already vegan. Add a shredded meat substitute sautéed with onions to marinara sauce. Slice and spread a vegan baguette with a paste of margarine, nutritional yeast, vegan parmesan, and fresh minced garlic or garlic powder.

*Veganize
Chocolate Cake
with Ice Cream*
To make the cake, substitute egg replacer for eggs, soymilk for milk, and margarine for butter. To make the frosting, substitute margarine for butter and a non-dairy cream for cream. To make ice cream, substitute cashew cream, soymilk, or non-dairy cream for dairy ingredients.

*Veganize
the All American
Grand Slam Breakfast*
Whip up a soy latte to get your brain ready for a day of creative vegan substitutions. Make tofu scrambled "eggs" with french toast or vegan pancakes, substituting margarine for butter, non-dairy milk or cashew cream for milk, and egg replacer for eggs. Serve with maple syrup and homemade or store-bought vegan "bacon" or vegan sausage links.

NOTHING

Is Beyond Veganizing

If it is edible, it can be made vegan.

Quiz: Which of the following can you purchase or find a recipe for on the internet?

A Gefilte fish is not found in any lake, stream, or ocean but only in cans, jars, and Jewish delicatessens. It is a morass of egg, flour, and carp in a jelly-like broth made from the head and bones of other fish. On so many levels it is simply wrong. So why would anyone want a vegan version? And if someone did, could they find it?

B Liver and onions. Two words—Hannibal Lecter.

C Black pudding is made from fresh blood, pearl barley, pig fat, onion, rusk, oatmeal, flour, and a blend of herbs and spices. It is popular in England and explains why Brits conquered half the world. They were looking for something edible to eat.

D Human flesh.

E All of the above.

Answer: E, *All of the above!* We are not kidding. No food is beyond veganizing. If you're craving it, you aren't the only one. Rest assured that someone, somewhere, has already veganized the food for which you've been pining and posted the recipe on the internet. Google is a vegan's best friend.

As for "D," the makers of Hufu stated:

"Our preliminary market research revealed the existence of a large segment of the public that was interested in the availability of a legal and healthy human flesh substitute, as well as vegetarians and vegans. We also found that Hufu is a great product for cannibals who want to quit. Hufu is also a great cannibal convenience food—no more Friday night hunting raids! Stay at home and enjoy the flavorful, convenient human flesh alternative."*

*Although Hufu turned out to be a hoax, many people ordered it showing there was a market for convenience foods that mimicked human flesh. Even cannibals want to go vegan!

The Vegetable Hater's Guide to Getting Your Daily Dose

Because we are vegan, people often assume we love vegetables. Not so. We dare to go where no vegan cookbook has gone before by making a shocking confession: vegetables are our least favorite food. We love fruit, and usually have several bowls filled with them on our kitchen counter, but vegetables are another matter entirely.

That said, we're not fools. We know that vegetables are an important part of a healthy diet, and so we have found a simple and quick way to ensure that we get our daily servings of veggies without having to taste them. It's our secret weapon in our war with the demands of nutrition: the juicer.

We cannot say that we enjoy the atrocious concoctions we force down every day. In fact, when we first started juicing, we had to build up a tolerance that gradually suppressed our gag reflexes. But we did overcome them, and now we can hand even our kids a glass of green, sludgy, and stinky juiced spinach, kale, beets, and cucumbers, and in a few big gulps, it's over. Then we can all move on with our day, highly nourished and guilt-free.

Helpful Hints:

Straws allow you to direct the juice to the back of the throat, bypassing the taste buds. We highly recommended them. Rinse and reuse for the planet's sake.

A glass of water nearby to rinse the mouth is also a plus. Swig, swallow, rinse, repeat.

If you hold your nose, or breathe only through your mouth for about 15 seconds after the last awful gulp, you can swallow the juice almost without tasting it at all.

A spoonful of sugar helps the medicine go down. Adding fruit to your veggies will sweeten the taste and make it more palatable.

The Devil is in the Details

The following lists the most common animal-derived ingredients in food products. Sadly, there are many more. For a comprehensive list, visit allamericanvegan.com.

Albumin or albumen
Egg whites.

Beeswax, royal jelly, propolis, honey, and bee pollen
Products derived from bees and their labor.

Carmine (also called cochineal or carminic acid)
Red dye made from crushed beetles.

Casein (also called calcium caseinate)
The predominant protein found in cow's milk. It is found in many cheese alternatives made from soy, rice, and almond. When choosing cheese, make sure it is labeled as vegan.

Collagen
A protein found almost exclusively in animals.

Elastin
A protein found in the connective tissue of animals.

Enzymes
Proteins added to foods in order to modify them. They can be animal, vegetable, bacterial, or fungal.

Gelatin
Derived from the collagen inside the skin and bones of animals. It is commonly used as a gelling agent in food, pharmaceuticals, photography, and cosmetic manufacturing.

Glycerin (also called glycerol and glycerides)
Viscous liquids derived from animals

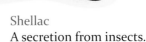

and often used in food and cosmetic production. However, there are vegan sources.

Isinglass
A fish extract commonly used to remove sediment from wines, beers, and other alcoholic beverages.

Keratin
Fibrous structural proteins that are the main component of products derived from the skin, such as hair, nails, claws, feathers, beaks, shells, and quills.

L-cysteine (also called cysteine or cystine)
A common dough conditioner derived from either vegetable or animal sources.

Lactose
Sugar found in cow's milk.

Lanolin
A greasy yellow substance secreted by the sebaceous glands of wool-bearing animals. It is commonly used in cosmetics and body products.

Natural Flavors
Can be vegetable or animal-derived.

Rennet
Enzymes acquired from the stomachs of slaughtered, unweaned baby cows for the production of cheese.

Shellac
A secretion from insects.

Sodium Sterol Lactylate
A mineral found in foods that can be animal or vegetable-derived.

Stearates (also called stearic acid)
Fatty acids derived from animals. However, there are a few vegan sources.

Refined or white sugar
May be processed using charred animal bones. For this reason, some vegans avoid it unless they know it is beet-derived, unrefined, or otherwise labeled as vegan-friendly.

Tallow
An animal fat.

Vitamin D3 (also called cholecalciferol)
A vitamin often derived from lanolin or fish oil.

Whey
The liquid that remains after milk has been curdled and strained to make cheese.

Me Tarzan, You Jane
Sex, Vegan Subterfuge, and the Reluctant Male

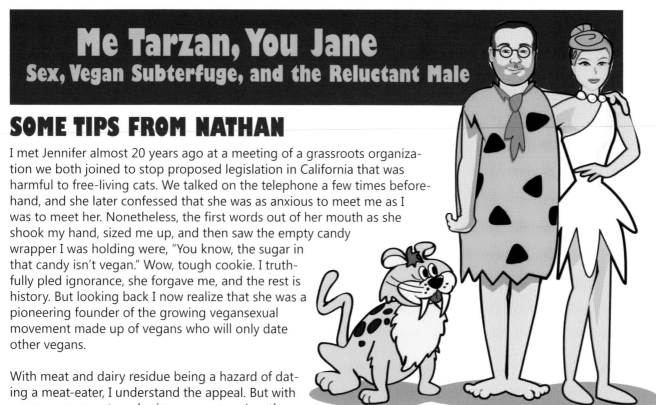

SOME TIPS FROM NATHAN

I met Jennifer almost 20 years ago at a meeting of a grassroots organization we both joined to stop proposed legislation in California that was harmful to free-living cats. We talked on the telephone a few times beforehand, and she later confessed that she was as anxious to meet me as I was to meet her. Nonetheless, the first words out of her mouth as she shook my hand, sized me up, and then saw the empty candy wrapper I was holding were, "You know, the sugar in that candy isn't vegan." Wow, tough cookie. I truthfully pled ignorance, she forgave me, and the rest is history. But looking back I now realize that she was a pioneering founder of the growing vegansexual movement made up of vegans who will only date other vegans.

With meat and dairy residue being a hazard of dating a meat-eater, I understand the appeal. But with vegan women outnumbering vegan men (another reason to go vegan, gents!), I do the math and worry. Are there enough male vegans to go around? For straight women and gay men who choose to date outside the faith, I say bring on the converts! Find a meat-eater with an open mind and a big heart (an unequivocal enthusiasm for cats is imperative), then roll up those sleeves and set about converting him. Here are some tips I hope will help.

For those who find themselves in a relationship with a man who has proven less than friendly to the vegan endeavor, take a lesson from the tom-cat. The average tom-cat has a roaming radius of about ten miles. Neuter the cat, place a bowl of kibble in your yard for him every day, and his wandering drops by 90%. He's lucky to go a mile. Why? Tom cats, like males of every species, are motivated by two things: food and sex. With a free meal and his balls removed, there is simply no reason to wander. He'll stay right here, thank you very much. Food and sex are inexorably linked. If your boyfriend or husband balks at the tofu and insists on the steak, withhold the sex. In no time at all he'll eat whatever the hell you put on his plate. It's that simple.

If that seems too harsh, or if abstinence isn't your thing, there is always subterfuge. How is it that some people who experience no squeamishness whatsoever about consuming body parts (a chicken's leg), ova (eggs), glandular secretions of animals (milk), and even coagulated secretions (cheese) suddenly become squealing cowards when you offer them products made from wheat protein or soybeans? Sometimes people need a little help in overcoming their irrational phobias. Take my father-in-law, for instance. Despite finding himself in a family in which vegans outnumber him and his fellow meat-eaters by a three-to-one margin, he remains suspicious of anything containing tofu or seitan.

About five years ago my mother-in-law surreptitiously switched from using ground meat in hamburger stroganoff, his favorite dish, to a vegan substitute, and he couldn't tell the difference. Had she been forthcoming about the exact nature of the "meat" in this dish, he might have refused to try it or made up his mind beforehand not to like it. Without that choice, his palate was none the wiser. After a while, my mother-in-law confessed, and he now freely admits that he enjoys a vegetarian version of his favorite dish on a weekly basis without ever asking, "Where's the beef?"

You Look Mahvelous

When you called your parents to explain that you are now vegan, your mom worried about your protein intake, asked if you could live without some favorite dish, and reminded you that you don't like vegetables so you will not get enough to eat. When you invited them over for dinner, there was a long silence on the other end of the line, but you could hear your dad in the background making a joke about stopping at a fast-food restaurant on the way over. While they relented and accepted your invitation, they were certain they were in for a bland, unappetizing meal.

Entertaining as a vegan often means battling low expectations. Before your family or friends walk in the door, they already think they know what the vegan dinner you've prepared for them will taste like and they've told each other to be polite regardless. Now is the time to give it the whole nine yards in order to win them over. Dim the lights, fire up a soy-based candle, download the latest Michael Bublé, and remember that the cutlery is placed from left to right in the order they are used, forks to the left of the plate, with knives and spoons on the right. Gents, no shirts with sports teams or band names and leave those cool, naturally-frayed jeans on the bedroom floor. The attire: business casual.

Food is *primarily* about taste, but it isn't *just* about taste. Food is an experience and like all experiences, the more complete it is, the more we enjoy it. A good, well-planned meal will appeal to all five senses: sight, hearing, touch, smell, and taste. It should look good, it should sound good, it should have good texture, it should smell good, and it should taste good. Fancy restaurants know this, which is why "fries with ketchup" becomes "organic hand-cut Yukon gold potatoes cooked in extra virgin cold-pressed Italian olive oil and served with Himalayan sea salt and an heirloom tomato preserve." Try selling "fries with ketchup" for $10. But already, we have decided that we are going to like it before the first forkful even enters our mouths. Yes, fork. We can't use our hands can we? It's too fancy.

And to look good, food should be served "by the clock" the way it is in upscale restaurants. That doesn't mean you have to have dinner at 6 p.m. It means when planning, preparing, and presenting meals to your guests, they should be situated on the plate according to type and place. There should be three items, the starch at 10 o'clock, the meat substitute at 2 o'clock and (dare we say it) the vegetable at 6 o'clock, even if all you are eating are a veggie burger, fries, and side salad.* The fries are at 10 o'clock, the burger is at 2 o'clock, and the salad is at 6 o'clock. Don't crowd and don't add more.

It will be colorful and it will be visually appealing, and that will go far in breaking down any prejudices about vegan food, allowing your guests to taste your offering with an open mind. Coupled with the fact that you dazzled them with the ambience and held your tongue during your dad's political tirade, they are likely to decide they love it before even trying it.

---

*To be more specific, a hand-carved seitan cutlet slow seasoned in a wild-harvested mushroom and yellow onion marinade, then flame grilled au jus, served on a fresh-baked artisan boule with romaine lettuce, vine-ripened tomato, sweet cucumber conserve, and aoli; along with organic mesclun greens of radicchio, chervil, and endive, served with plum tomatoes in a reduction of oak-aged balsamic vinegar with hints of fresh-cracked black peppercorns and topped with cubed, seasoned, and toasted sourdough accompaniments.

IMPORTANT MOMENTS IN VEGAN HISTORY

15,000 BCE
LASCAUX, FRANCE
FIRST VEGETARIAN OPENS
FIRST GENERATION GAP

Tween cave girl chides father returning from hunt, tells mother preparing carcass: "I hope you don't expect me to eat that poor mammoth." Retreats to dark cave in protest, spends time painting pretty pictures of animals on walls.

5000 BCE
INDIA
BUDDHISM

Siddhartha Gautama tells followers, "Harm no living thing" and means it! Chinese restaurants worldwide add "vegetarian" sections to their menus.

10,000 BCE
MESOPOTAMIA
CULTIVATION OF CROPS

The first permanent villages emerge as hunting/gathering is replaced by farming. Man can now live on bread alone.

1000 BCE
CHINA
FIRST CELEBRITY CHEF

Chinese servant accidentally cooks soybeans too long and is forced to serve coagulated bean curd to his master. Fearful of ensuing whipping, cowering servant is instead hailed as "genius," and the other "other white meat" is born.

IMPORTANT MOMENTS IN VEGAN HISTORY

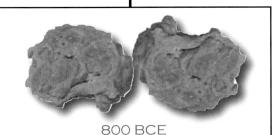

800 BCE
JAPAN
DISCOVERY OF SEITAN

The alternative to tofu's hegemony leads to civil war in the vegetarian community. China sticks with tofu; Japan embraces seitan. Ancient vegetarian pacifist calls for calm: "Can't we all just get along?"

500
EUROPE
PROTO-HIPPIES

The hippies of their age, medieval monks live simple, communal lives in monasteries and keep the hallmarks of civilization—reading, writing, and vegetarianism—alive during the Dark Ages.

49 BCE
ROMAN EMPIRE
"VENI, VIDI, VEGAN."

After pacing the riverbank in reflective deliberation, Julius Caesar decides to give up meat, eggs, and dairy products, and crosses the Rubicon river to eat at Fabrizio's Vegan Pasta House, renown throughout the Roman Empire for its delicious soy-meatball sub. The phrase "Crossing the Rubicon" becomes synonymous with decisive change.

1000
ENGLAND
THE ART OF VEGETARIAN SUBSTITUTION

Forbidden to hunt on the lands of their feudal lords, peasants invent the art of vegetarian substitution, and "Welsh Rabbit," a cheese-and-beer sauce over toast, is born. Peasants, who make up the majority of the European population, are largely vegetarian, though not necessarily by choice.

IMPORTANT MOMENTS IN VEGAN HISTORY

The Enlightenment takes Europe by storm, setting the stage for future social revolutions worldwide, including animal rights. Historians trace its origin to René Descartes' Discourse on the Method. The full title was Discourse on the Method of Substituting Seitan and Tofu for the Meat of Animals in Everyday Recipes. *It's a cookbook!*

The Black Plague sweeps over Europe, killing one-third of the population and hastening the end of feudalism. The resulting labor shortage hikes wages and decreases social stratification, leading to more meat-eating.

Martin Luther posts his 95 Theses on the door of Castle Church, sparking the Protestant Reformation. Little known to historians, one of his complaints was the addition of the ingredient "whey" in the otherwise vegan communion wafer. "Mean to cows," he is heard mumbling as he nails his list of gripes to the door.

Important Moments in Vegan History

DECEMBER 16, 1773
BOSTON, MASSACHUSETTS
BOSTON TEA PARTY

American colonists dressed as Native Americans pour British tea into Boston Harbor, protesting the Crown's tax on the soymilk that allowed them to enjoy their tea free of cruelty, cholesterol, hormones, and antibiotics. "Give me non-dairy creamer or give me death!" proclaim the patriots.

1950s
UNITED STATES
U.S. GOVERNMENT
PROPAGANDA

Under pressure from the meat, egg, and dairy industries, the USDA introduces "The Four Food Groups" in schools nation-wide. Generations of Americans are duped into eating too much fat, protein, and cholesterol "for their own good."

Main Entry: **veg·an**
Pronunciation: \ˈvē-gən also ˈvā- also
ˈve-jən or -ˌjan\
Function: noun
Etymology: by contraction from vegetarian
Date: 1944
: a strict vegetarian who consumes no
meat, eggs, or dairy products; also: one who
abstains from using animal products (as
leather, fur, wool, or silk)

1944
ENGLAND
SO *THAT'S* WHAT IT'S CALLED!

The term "vegan" is coined by the newly formed Vegan Society. Using the first three and last two letters of the word "vegetarian," they oppose eating dairy products and eggs, arguing that vegan is the first and last word on what it means to be a vegetarian. Hens and cows on dairy farms worldwide celebrate as the vegetarian movement, embracing veganism, brings them into its protection.

IMPORTANT MOMENTS IN VEGAN HISTORY

1967
SAN FRANCISCO, CALIFORNIA
SUMMER OF LOVE

Vegetarianism becomes more widespread (though tasteless) as hippies descend on Haight-Ashbury in San Francisco and declare that all you need is love, brown rice, and steamed vegetables.

JULY 20, 1969
THE MOON
CHEESE TAKES A HIT

Neil Armstrong walks on the moon and confirms it is *not* made of cheese.

1981
UNITED STATES
KEEPIN' IT SIMPLE

Vegetarian "protein combining" disproven. Vegetarians once again free to eat beans without rice and rice without beans.

1981
UNITED STATES
KETCHUPGATE

In a victory for processed vegetables, Ronald Reagan declares ketchup a vegetable. Who knew?

IMPORTANT MOMENTS IN VEGAN HISTORY

1980s
ENGLAND
MAD COW DISEASE

Bloody hell! Many British gobsmacked into becoming vegetarians as meat-eating is linked to madness.

1989
UNITED STATES
FIRST ANIMATED VEGETARIAN

Lisa Simpson, the middle child and conscience of the Simpson family, proclaims that she is a vegetarian for ethical reasons.

1990s
UNITED STATES
NATURAL FOOD STORES COME OF AGE

Vegans recycle their dusters, no longer having to contend with dust-covered cans of veggie links for sale in the back of smelly vitamin stores.

1988
UNITED STATES
BEEF: IT'S WHAT'S CLOGGING YOUR ARTERIES

Beef industry spokesperson James Garner has quintuple heart bypass surgery.

IMPORTANT MOMENTS IN VEGAN HISTORY

1991
OAKLAND, CALIFORNIA
HITTIN' ONE FOR THE CRITTERS

Fans enjoying the American pastime forgo animal cruelty, carcinogenic nitrates, and hormones found in hot dogs as the Oakland A's stadium begins offering veggie dogs and veggie burgers. Other stadiums soon follow suit.

LATE 1990s
UNITED STATES
WHAT'S IN, OR NOT IN, A NAME?

Vegan labels begin appearing on food packages.

LATE 1990s
UNITED STATES
ONE GIANT LEAP FOR SOYMILK

Starbucks introduces soymilk to the masses. And they like it!

1992
UNITED STATES
A SLIPPERY SLOPE FOR MEAT, EGGS, AND DAIRY

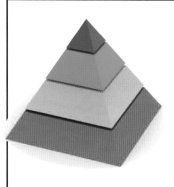

The "Four Food Groups" is dropped in favor of a food pyramid. Meat, eggs, and dairy products pushed one step closer to oblivion.

IMPORTANT MOMENTS IN VEGAN HISTORY

2000s
UNITED STATES
BEEN THERE, DONE THAT

Sex, drugs, and rock-n-roll already taken, rebellious teens stick it to the man by becoming vegan and demanding their veggies. Number of vegetarian teens triples.

EVOLUTION OF THE AMERICAN TEENAGER

SEX, DRUGS, ROCK N' ROLL AND VEGETABLES

2000s
UNITED STATES
MEAT CONSUMPTION
LINKED TO IMPOTENCE

More men become vegetarian, doing it for the "chicks."

2000s
BIRDS OF A FEATHER
FLOCK TOGETHER

The "vegansexual" movement begins, removing the most eligible bachelors and bachelorettes from the general dating pool.

2011
UNITED STATES

All American Vegan is published. ;-)

2000s
UNITED STATES
GIVE THE PEOPLE WHAT THEY WANT

Vegan analogs of traditional American comfort foods come of age.

ONE WEEK MENU PLANNER

Becoming a vegan is like going for a swim. There are two ways to immerse yourself. You can enter slowly and timidly, inch by inch, delaying your acclimation; or you can jump right in, doing a cannonball off the high board and adjusting to the water temperature right away. "Come on, it's not that cold!" you get to yell at the sissies dipping their toes in at the edge of the pool. And it's true, isn't it? Once you're fully submerged, it isn't that cold after all. The same is true of being vegan. It's not as hard as it looks, once you get the hang of it.

That's how we both became vegan—cold "tofurkey"—and we highly recommend it. It forces you to experiment with new foods and expand your options, which in the long run makes being vegan easier.

When we made the transition, guides to vegan living didn't exist, and so it was through a process of trial and error that we discovered which ingredients were vegan and which weren't, which vegan foods were delicious and which weren't, and how to substitute vegan for non-vegan ingredients when cooking and baking. What we wouldn't have given for what we're giving you!

Following is a one week menu planner that includes a vegan breakfast, lunch, snack, dinner, and dessert for every day of the week. It is for the aspiring vegan who wants to jump right into veganism, to really make a splash. It's all here, a week's worth of our favorite recipes and ready-made foods—everything you need for a crash course in vegan shopping and cooking, everything you need to launch the new vegan you.

SUPERSIZE Me!

A recent study suggests that many Americans eat by the clock, at 8:00 a.m., 12:00 p.m., and 6:00 p.m.— that is, at breakfast, lunch, and dinner time—whether or not they are hungry. For these people dining isn't about filling a void; it's about experiencing food. We have a sneaking suspicion that these are the people for whom the Denny's Grand Slam breakfast was designed, people who like to have dinner for breakfast. For them we offer the "All American Breakfast" option. For those with a more European relationship with food, we offer the "Continental Breakfast," of leaner fare. Likewise, we realize that our suggested daily snack choice might be calorie overload given the main dishes and the desserts offered. But we include it nonetheless to show the wide variety of vegan analogs of traditional American snacks. It is included for readers who squeal with delight at finding the maraschino cherry covered in heavy syrup in their canned fruit cocktail (you know who you are). Veganism can accommodate your palate and your appetite too. If, on the other hand, you are interested in a healthy afternoon snack, we simply suggest you try fruit. Quick, easy, healthy, and of course vegan!

Note: Recipes for many of the items in the following One Week Menu Planner can be found in this cookbook. For ready-made items, such as candy bars and non-dairy yogurt, there are brand-name product recommendations at allamericanvegan.com.

A week of American

Monday

ALL AMERICAN BREAKFAST
Pancakes with whipped sweet butter, hash browns, and not "bacon" strips

CONTINENTAL BREAKFAST
English muffin, non-dairy yogurt, and a latte

LUNCH
No tuna fish sandwich and potato chips

SNACK
Candy bar

DINNER
Fried no chicken, buttermilk biscuits, mashed potatoes, and gravy

DESSERT
Ice cream sundae

Tuesday

ALL AMERICAN BREAKFAST
French toast and not sausages

CONTINENTAL BREAKFAST
Slice of peanut butter coffee cake

LUNCH
No BLT sandwich and potato salad

SNACK
Ice cream bar

DINNER
Lasagna, garlic bread, and a Caesar salad

DESSERT
Chocolate layer cake

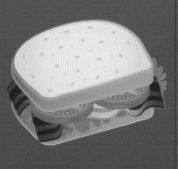

Wednesday

ALL AMERICAN BREAKFAST
Glazed donuts with soymilk

CONTINENTAL BREAKFAST
Toast with margarine or jam and a bowl of cereal with non-dairy milk

LUNCH
No chicken noodle soup with crackers

SNACK
Golden cream filled sponge cake

DINNER
Philly cheese steak, onion rings, and a salad with Thousand Island dressing

DESSERT
New York cheesecake

meals, *veganized*

Thursday

ALL AMERICAN BREAKFAST
Scrambled no eggs, not "bacon" strips, and toast

CONTINENTAL BREAKFAST
Fruit smoothie

LUNCH
Club sandwich and french fries

SNACK
Chocolate chip cookies

DINNER
No chicken pot pie and salad with Ranch dressing

DESSERT
Apple pie à la mode

Friday

ALL AMERICAN BREAKFAST
Omelet with hash browns and toast

CONTINENTAL BREAKFAST
Cinnamon roll

LUNCH
Buffalo strips and coleslaw

SNACK
Nachos

DINNER
Hamburger, tater tots, corn on the cob, and a milkshake

DESSERT
Chocolate pudding

Saturday

ALL AMERICAN BREAKFAST
Breakfast hash

CONTINENTAL BREAKFAST
Blueberry muffin

LUNCH
Grilled cheese sandwich or tuna melt and macaroni salad

SNACK
Ice cream cone

DINNER
BBQ no ribs, cornbread, and vegan baked beans

DESSERT
Banana cream pie

End Your First Week as

SUNDAY BRUNCH

You're Invited!

To celebrate my first week as a vegan!

Sunday Brunch
11:00

Congratulations!

Your first week as a vegan deserves a celebration! Invite your friends and family over, make our suggested brunch menu, and dispel all their preconceived notions about vegan food. Who knows, maybe this occasion will be the one that inspires one of your friends—the first of many— to follow your amazing example and go vegan, too.

a Vegan with a BANG!

SundayVeganBrunch
M E N U

FRENCH TOAST 78
SCRAMBLED NO EGGS 82
PEANUT BUTTER COFFEE CAKE 75
DANISHES 72
NO CHICKEN FINGERS 96
WITH DIPPING SAUCES 118, 125
NO TUNA FISH SALAD ON CRACKERS 33
WALDORF SALAD 158
NEW YORK CHEESECAKE 138
GEL-OH! PARFAIT 141

ALL AMERICAN VEGAN

Breakfast
Served All Day

Cinnamon Rolls 70
Blueberry Muffins 71
Danishes 72
Banana Nut Bread 73
Glazed Donuts 74
Peanut Butter Coffee Cake 75
Pecan Rolls 76

Breakfast Hash 77
French Toast 78
Omelet 79
Pancakes 80
Not Sausages 81
Scrambled No Eggs 82
Not "Bacon" Strips 32

Lunch & Dinner

No BLT 84
Club Sandwich 85
Philly Cheese Steak 86
Grilled Cheese Sandwich 87
Reuben Sandwich 88

No Tuna Fish Sandwich 89
No Tuna Melt 89
No Egg Salad Sandwich 90
Sloppy Joes 91
Hamburger 92
BBQ No Ribs 93

No Chicken Pot Pie 94
Corndogs 95
Fried No Chicken 96
Macaroni and Cheese 97
Pizza 98
Lasagna 99

Sides

Soups

No Chicken Noodle Soup 102
Cream of Mushroom Soup 103
Matzo Ball Soup 104

Appetizers & Sides

French Fries 105
Onion Rings 106
Mozzarella Sticks 107
Garlic Bread 108
Mashed Potatoes 109
Buffalo Strips 110
Buttermilk Biscuits 111
Cornbread 112
Nachos 113
Potato Salad 114
Coleslaw 115
Macaroni Salad 116
No Chicken Fingers 96

Dressings & Sauces

Caesar Salad Dressing 117
Ranch Dip and Dressing 118
Thousand Island Dressing 119
Not So Secret Sauce 120
Tartar Sauce 121
Warm Fruit Topping 122
Whipped Sweet Butter 123
Gravy 124
BBQ Sauce 125
Parmesan 126

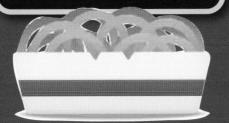

Desserts

Pies

Apple Pie 128
Cherry Pie 129
Banana Cream Pie 130
Coconut Cream Pie 131
Peanut Butter Pie 132
Chocolate Cream Pie 139
Chocolate Banana Cream Pie 139

Cookies

Chocolate Chip Cookies 133
Peanut Butter Cookies 134

Cakes

Chocolate Layer Cake 135
Golden Cream Filled Spongecakes 136
Vanilla Cupcakes 137
New York Cheesecake 138

Ice Creams

Vanilla Ice Cream 142
Chocolate Ice Cream 143
Strawberry Ice Cream 144
Milkshake 145
Root Beer Float 145
Ice Cream Sundae 145

Other Treats

Chocolate Pudding 139
Peanut Butter Cups 140
Gel-oh! Parfait 141
Cookie Pudding Parfait 139
Chocolate Sauce 146
Pie Crust 147
Coconut & Tofu Whipped Topping 148-149

Let your mouse lead you to the best vegan cheese

The latest and greatest vegan convenience foods are just a few clicks away

Many of the recipes in this book are quick and easy. But you can make them even easier. You want a vegan pizza but don't want to spend time kneading the dough and letting it rise? No problem. You can buy the ready-made vegan pizza crust, pizza sauce, and the grated vegan cheese. In fact, you can buy a frozen vegan pizza with all the trimmings! Just heat and serve.

Because new products are coming out all the time, we have intentionally omitted any product references in this cookbook. The companion website identifies our favorite ready-made vegan food products by brand-name. So before you try our recipes, check it out. And while you're there, check out our blog, information about vegan living, materials for vegan activists, and much more.

allamericanvegan.com
Get a taste of what you won't be missing

BREAKFAST

Breakfast

CINNAMON ROLLS

Makes 12-15

INGREDIENTS

For Dough
- 2 tsp. (1 packet) active dry yeast
- 1 Tbs. plus ¼ cup vegan sugar, divided
- ½ cup warm water
- ½ cup non-dairy milk
- ⅓ cup melted but cooled* vegan margarine
- 1 tsp. salt
- reconstituted egg replacer powder equal to 1 egg
- 3¾ cups all-purpose flour

For Filling
- ¼ cup softened margarine plus more to grease pan
- ⅔ cup vegan brown sugar
- 2 Tbs. ground cinnamon
- optional:
    - ¾ cup raisins or chopped walnuts

For Glaze
- ⅓ cup vegan margarine
- 2 cups vegan powdered sugar
- 1½ tsp. vanilla
- 2 Tbs. hot water

Cool or yeast could deactivate.

TO PREPARE

Dough: Dissolve yeast and 1 Tbs. sugar in warm water and let stand for 5-10 minutes to proof (yeast should foam).

Separately, combine milk, ¼ cup sugar, margarine, salt, and egg replacer. Then combine this mixture with dissolved yeast and flour, mixing to make a dough.

Turn dough onto a lightly floured surface and knead for 5 minutes, dusting with more flour as needed to prevent sticking.

Place dough in a well-greased bowl, flip, cover with a damp kitchen towel or plastic wrap and let rise for 1½ hours.

Punch dough down and roll out on a lightly floured surface into a 15 x 9 inch rectangle.

Filling: Spread margarine evenly over dough. Combine brown sugar and cinnamon in a bowl and then sprinkle evenly over dough. Sprinkle with optional raisins or walnuts.

Grease a large baking pan with margarine.

Beginning at the 15 inch side, roll up dough to end and pinch to seal. Cut into 12 to 15 slices, approximately 1 inch thick. Place cinnamon roll slices close together (½ inch apart) on the pan. Cover with a tea towel or cloth napkin and let rise for 1 hour.

Bake rolls at 400 degrees for 10-15 minutes until golden brown.

Glaze: While rolls are baking, whip all glaze ingredients together until smooth. Spread evenly over rolls.

BLUEBERRY MUFFINS

Makes 1 dozen

INGREDIENTS

- 2 cups all-purpose flour
- ¼ cup vegan sugar
- 1 tsp. baking powder
- 1 tsp. baking soda
- ½ tsp. salt
- ¼ cup canola oil
- 1 cup maple syrup
- 1 cup non-dairy milk
- 1½ tsp. apple cider vinegar
- 1¼ cups fresh or frozen blueberries

TO PREPARE

Preheat oven to 350 degrees.

Grease a muffin pan or line with paper baking cups.

In a large bowl, combine flour, sugar, baking powder, baking soda, and salt.

Separately, whisk oil, maple syrup, milk, and vinegar together until foamy.

Combine dry and wet ingredients, mixing to make a batter. Then gently fold in blueberries.

Pour batter into muffin pan or cups.

Bake for 15-20 minutes, or until a toothpick inserted in the center comes out clean.

Allow to cool before serving. Spread with whipped sweet butter (recipe, p. 123).

DANISHES

Makes 1 dozen

INGREDIENTS

For Dough
- 2 tsp. (1 packet) active dry yeast
- 4 Tbs. plus ¼ cup vegan sugar, divided
- 1 cup warm water
- 3½ cups all-purpose flour, divided
- ½ cup canola oil
- 1 tsp. salt

For Fruit Topping
- vegan fruit jam or warmed fruit topping (recipe, p. 122)

For Creamy Tofu Topping
- ½ cup water
- ¼ cup canola oil
- 1 cup firm silken tofu
- ½ tsp. lemon juice
- ½ cup vegan sugar
- ¼ tsp. salt
- 2 Tbs. all-purpose flour

- vegan margarine for brushing, melted but cooled*

Cool or yeast could deactivate.

TO PREPARE

Dough: Dissolve yeast and 1 Tbs. sugar in warm water and let stand for 5-10 minutes to proof (yeast should foam).

Combine dissolved yeast, 2 cups flour, and 3 Tbs. of sugar, stirring to make a sticky dough.

Place dough in a well-greased bowl, flip, and cover with a damp kitchen towel or plastic wrap and let rise for 1 hour.

Separately, combine oil, salt, and ¼ cup sugar, then mix into dough.

Mix in remaining 1½ cups flour. Knead for 5 minutes, dusting with more flour as needed to prevent sticking.

Place dough in a well-greased bowl, flip, cover with a damp kitchen towel or plastic wrap and let rise for 1 hour. Meanwhile, prepare toppings.

Fruit topping: If you are using warmed fruit topping instead of jam, prepare.

Creamy tofu topping: Blend all tofu topping ingredients together in a blender or food processor. Transfer to saucepan and cook over medium-low heat, stirring constantly until thickened, about 5 minutes. Allow to cool.

Danishes: Roll out dough on a lightly floured surface to ⅛ inch thick, brush with melted margarine and then cut into 4 inch squares. Place squares on a greased or parchment paper-lined baking sheet.

Place a dollop of 1 Tbs. creamy tofu topping in the center of
continued...

each square. Then place a slightly smaller dollop of fruit topping or jam in the center of the creamy tofu topping.

Bring 2 opposite edges of square to center and pinch together. Fold remaining corners ½ inch toward the center.

Cover with a tea towel or cloth napkin and let rise for 20 minutes.

Bake 15 minutes at 350 degrees or until golden brown, brushing with more margarine 3 minutes before they are done.

BANANA NUT BREAD

Makes 1 loaf

INGREDIENTS

- 2 cups all-purpose flour
- 2 tsp. baking powder
- ½ tsp. baking soda
- 1 tsp. egg replacer powder
- ¾ tsp. salt
- 1 cup vegan sugar
- 2 medium bananas, mashed
- ½ cup non-dairy milk
- ½ cup canola oil or melted vegan margarine
- 1 tsp. vanilla
- 1 cup chopped walnuts

TO PREPARE

Preheat oven to 350 degrees.

Grease and flour loaf pan.

In a large bowl, combine flour, baking powder, baking soda, egg replacer powder, and salt.

Separately, combine sugar, bananas, milk, oil or margarine, and vanilla.

Combine wet and dry ingredients, mixing to make a batter.

Fold in chopped nuts.

Bake for 25 minutes, then lightly cover with foil to prevent top and edges from overbrowning, and bake for another 20-25 minutes, or until a toothpick inserted into the center of loaf comes out clean.

Serve with whipped sweet butter (recipe, p. 123).

GLAZED DONUTS

INGREDIENTS

Makes 1 dozen

For Dough
- 4 tsp. (2 packets) active dry yeast
- 1 tsp. plus ¼ cup vegan sugar, divided
- ⅓ cup warm water
- ½ cup non-dairy milk
- ⅓ cup melted but cooled* vegan margarine
- reconstituted egg replacer powder equal to 2 eggs, beaten for 2 minutes
- 3 cups all-purpose flour
- 1½ tsp. salt

For Glaze
- ⅓ cup melted vegan margarine
- 2 cups vegan powdered sugar
- 1½ tsp. vanilla
- 2 Tbs. water

- canola oil for deep frying

*Cool or yeast could deactivate.

TO PREPARE

Dough: Dissolve yeast and 1 tsp. sugar in warm water and let stand for 5-10 minutes to proof (yeast should foam).

In a large bowl, combine milk, margarine, and ¼ cup sugar.

Mix in beaten egg replacer and dissolved yeast. Add in flour and salt, mixing to make a dough.

Turn dough onto a lightly floured surface and knead for 3 minutes, dusting with more flour as needed to prevent sticking.

Place dough in a well-greased bowl, flip, and cover with a damp kitchen towel or plastic wrap and let rise for 1½ hours.

Punch dough down and roll out on a lightly floured surface to ½ inch thick.

Cut out donut shapes with donut cutter (or use rim of one regular drinking glass to cut out donut, then a shot-glass to cut out the center hole). Place donuts on a parchment paper-lined baking sheet. Cover with a tea towel or cloth napkin and let rise for 1 hour.

Glaze: While donuts are rising, whip all glaze ingredients together until smooth. Set aside.

Prepare plate lined with paper towels to receive donuts after frying to absorb excess oil. Also prepare a raised wire rack to place donuts on after glazing so that excess glaze can drain off without soaking the bottom of the donuts.

Fry donuts in oil heated to 350 degrees, turning once to cook
continued...

both sides until golden brown. Be prepared, they will cook very quickly. Remove to paper towels.

When donuts are still warm but cool enough to handle, dip in glaze, twisting them as you remove in order to ensure a thick coating. Place on wire rack. Allow glaze to solidify before serving.

PEANUT BUTTER COFFEE CAKE

Serves 6

INGREDIENTS

For Topping
- ½ cup packed vegan brown sugar
- ¾ cup all-purpose flour
- ¼ cup roasted & salted creamy peanut butter
- 4 Tbs. vegan margarine

For Cake
- 2 cups all-purpose flour
- 2 tsp. baking powder
- ½ tsp. baking soda
- ½ tsp. salt
- 1 cup non-dairy milk
- 1 cup packed vegan brown sugar
- ½ tsp. roasted & salted creamy peanut butter
- 1 tsp. vanilla
- reconstituted egg replacer powder equal to 2 eggs
- ¼ cup vegan margarine, softened

TO PREPARE

Preheat oven to 375 degrees.

Grease and flour an 8 x 12 inch baking pan.

Topping: Mix brown sugar and flour. Cut in peanut butter and margarine until you have a crumbly topping. Set aside.

Cake: In a large bowl, combine flour, baking powder, baking soda, and salt.

Separately, blend milk, brown sugar, peanut butter, vanilla, egg replacer, and margarine.

Combine dry and wet ingredients, mixing to make a batter.

Pour batter into baking pan.

Sprinkle topping evenly over the batter.

Bake for 25-30 minutes, or until a toothpick inserted into the center comes out clean.

Allow to cool before serving.

PECAN ROLLS

Makes 12-15

INGREDIENTS

For Dough
- 2 tsp. (1 packet) active dry yeast
- 1 Tbs. plus ¼ cup vegan sugar, divided
- ½ cup warm water
- ½ cup non-dairy milk
- ⅓ cup melted but cooled* vegan margarine
- 1 tsp. salt
- reconstituted egg replacer powder equal to 1 egg
- 3¾ cups all-purpose flour

For Filling
- ¼ cup plus 2 Tbs. more softened vegan margarine, divided
- 1 cup vegan brown sugar
- 1 cup chopped pecans

Cool or yeast could deactivate.

TO PREPARE

Dough: Dissolve yeast and 1 Tbs. sugar in warm water and let stand for 5-10 minutes to proof (yeast should foam).

Separately, combine milk, ¼ cup sugar, margarine, salt, and egg replacer. Then combine this mixture with dissolved yeast and flour, mixing to make a dough.

Turn dough onto a lightly floured surface and knead for 5 minutes, dusting with more flour as needed to prevent sticking.

Place in a well-greased bowl, flip, cover with a damp kitchen towel or plastic wrap and let rise for 1½ hours.

Punch dough down and roll out on a lightly floured surface into a 15 x 9 inch rectangle.

Filling: Spread ¼ cup margarine evenly over dough. Combine brown sugar and pecans together in a bowl and then sprinkle half of it evenly over dough.

Coat the bottom and sides of a large baking dish with remaining 2 Tbs. margarine and sprinkle remaining brown sugar-pecan mixture on the bottom of the pan.

Beginning at the 15 inch side, roll up dough to end and pinch to seal. Cut into 12 to 15 slices, approximately 1 inch thick. Place slices close together (½ inch apart) in the baking dish. Cover with a tea towel or cloth napkin and let rise for 1 hour.

Bake rolls at 400 degrees for 10-15 minutes or until golden brown.

continued...

After removing from oven, flip rolls out onto a serving plate. This will turn them right side up. Scoop out any pecans remaining in pan and use them to cover any bare spots.

Best served warm.

BREAKFAST HASH

INGREDIENTS

Serves 4

- ¼ cup diced onion
- ½ cup sliced mushrooms
- 4 Tbs. vegan margarine, divided
- 2 cups (cut into ½ inch chunks) store-bought seitan or homemade no chicken seitan cutlets (recipe, p. 34)
- 2 medium or 1 large potato, baked or microwaved, peeled, and cut into ½ inch chunks
- 2 cups precooked white rice
- ½ cup nutritional yeast
- ½ tsp. garlic powder
- black pepper to taste
- ⅛ cup soy sauce

TO PREPARE

Sauté onion and mushrooms in 2 Tbs. margarine until tender.

Add seitan, potato, and 2 more Tbs. margarine. Sauté until the mixture begins to crisp.

Add precooked rice, nutritional yeast, garlic powder, black pepper, and soy sauce. Stir to combine.

Flatten mixture with the back of a spatula into hash brown shape.

Cook over medium-low heat until crispy, then flip and crisp other side.

Allow to cool for a few minutes before serving with ketchup or vegan hot sauce.

Breakfast

FRENCH TOAST

Serves 2

INGREDIENTS

- 1⅓ cups cashew cream (recipe, p. 39) or vegan non-dairy cream
- 1 tsp. vanilla
- ¼ tsp. salt
- 1 Tbs. vegan sugar
- ⅓ cup all-purpose flour
- 1 tsp. cinnamon
- 4 slices vegan bread
- 2 Tbs. vegan margarine

TO PREPARE

Combine cream, vanilla, salt, sugar, flour, and cinnamon in a blender.

Pour mixture into shallow pan.

Place bread slices in mixture. After 2 minutes, flip bread to other side and soak for 1 minute more. Bread becomes weak from soaking and may need to be handled with a spatula.

Heat margarine in pan.

When skillet is hot and margarine melted, place bread in pan and cook over medium heat until bottom is golden brown and partially crispy.

Flip bread and cook other side until golden brown and partially crispy, too.

Serve hot with warm maple syrup, whipped sweet butter (recipe, p. 123), warmed fruit topping (recipe, p. 122).

OMELET

Makes 3

INGREDIENTS

Filling for *Each* Omelet
- ¼ cup grated vegan cheese
- ⅛ cup sautéed mushrooms
- ⅛ cup sautéed onions

For Batter
- 1½ cups (1 package) firm silken tofu
- 8 slices store-bought vegan turkey
- 3 Tbs. cashew cream (recipe, p. 39) or vegan non-dairy cream
- 2 Tbs. nutritional yeast
- 1½ tsp. egg replacer powder
- ½ tsp. tahini
- ⅛ tsp. onion powder
- 1 tsp. turmeric

- 1 tsp. vegan margarine per omelet to grease the pan

TO PREPARE

Filling: Prepare filling ingredients and set aside.

Batter: Combine all batter ingredients in a food processor until smooth.

Melt margarine in skillet over medium heat. When skillet is hot and margarine melted, spoon ⅓ batter onto skillet. Spread out with the back of spoon, creating a circle that is as thin as possible.

Spread fillings evenly in omelet, with grated cheese being the bottom (first) layer.

Cover and cook for 4-5 minutes over medium-low heat. When the edges have dried out, and when by gently lifting a corner with a spatula you can see that the bottom of the omelet is thoroughly cooked and golden brown, slide spatula under omelet from all directions to loosen. Then gently flip one side of omelet onto other, making a half circle. Be sure to wipe your spatula between uses, as this will make moving and flipping the omelet easier.

Cook for 1 additional minute, uncovered. Then flip and cook other side for a few minutes more. If you have trouble flipping and the omelet falls to pieces, it may not look as pretty, but it will taste the same! Flip pieces in pan to ensure even cooking, and call it a scramble.

Carefully lift onto plate to serve. Enough batter remains to make 2 more omelets.

Serve with a side of hash browns, not sausages (recipe, p. 81), not bacon strips (recipe, p. 32), and/or toast.

PANCAKES

Serves 4

INGREDIENTS

- 2 cups all-purpose flour
- 2 Tbs. vegan sugar
- 2 Tbs. baking powder
- ¼ tsp. salt
- 2 cups non-dairy milk
- 4 Tbs. canola oil plus more to grease the pan

TO PREPARE

In a large bowl, combine flour, sugar, baking powder, and salt.

Add milk and oil and beat until batter is almost entirely smooth (a few tiny lumps are actually preferable).

Lightly oil pan, wiping away excess with a paper towel.

To test pan for readiness, sprinkle with a few drops of water. When bubbles skitter, pan is ready.

Pour approximately ⅓ cup batter (or enough for whatever size pancakes you prefer) into pan.

Flip after pancakes fluff and are golden brown on pan side, about 3 minutes.

Cook other side until it is also golden brown, about 2 minutes.

Serve hot with warm maple syrup, whipped sweet butter (recipe, p. 123), and/or warmed fruit topping (recipe, p. 122).

NOT SAUSAGES

Makes 8

INGREDIENTS

- 2½ cups wheat gluten flour
- ¼ cup garbanzo flour
- ½ cup nutritional yeast
- 2 Tbs. onion powder
- 2 tsp. coarse-grind black pepper
- 2 tsp. paprika
- ½ tsp. cayenne
- 1 tsp. smoked paprika
- ½ tsp. dried oregano
- 1 tsp. salt
- ⅛ tsp. ground allspice
- *optional:* 1 Tbs. fennel seed
- 2¼ cups vegan chicken or vegetable broth
- 4 tsp. minced garlic
- 2 Tbs. canola or olive oil
- 2 Tbs. soy sauce
- 2 tsp. liquid smoke hickory seasoning

TO PREPARE

In a large bowl, combine wheat gluten, garbanzo flour, nutritional yeast, onion powder, black pepper, paprika, cayenne, smoked paprika, oregano, salt, allspice, and optional fennel seed.

Separately, combine broth, garlic, oil, soy sauce, and hickory seasoning.

Combine wet and dry ingredients, mixing to make a dough.

Knead for 2 minutes.

Cut seitan into 8 even sized chunks. Shape chunks into sausages. Wrap loosely in parchment paper or cheesecloth, followed by aluminum foil.

Place not sausages in a steamer basket within a large stockpot containing water (filled to below the level of the not sausages) and cook for 1 hour, adding more water as needed to ensure a constant supply of steam.

When cool enough to handle, unwrap not sausages and sauté in oil or margarine until crispy before serving.

Serve as a breakfast side dish or use as filling for corndogs (recipe, p. 95).

SCRAMBLED NO EGGS

Serves 3

INGREDIENTS

- ½ cup cashew cream (recipe, p. 39)
- 2 Tbs. nutritional yeast
- ½ tsp. salt
- ½ tsp. garlic powder
- ½ tsp. mustard powder
- ¼ tsp. black pepper
- ½ cup diced yellow onion
- 3 Tbs. vegan margarine
- 1½ cups firm crumbled tofu

TO PREPARE

Whisk together cream, nutritional yeast, salt, garlic powder, mustard powder, and black pepper. Set aside.

Sauté onion in margarine until tender.

Add tofu and cook over medium heat, without stirring, until tofu starts to crisp. Flip tofu and crisp again.

Pour liquid ingredients into pan. Stir to coat tofu. Then cook, stirring occasionally and scraping bottom of pan, until enough moisture has evaporated to attain consistency of scrambled eggs.

Serve hot with ketchup or vegan hot sauce.

LUNCH & DINNER

Lunch & Dinner

NO BLT

Makes 4

INGREDIENTS

- 1 package store-bought vegan "bacon" or 1 batch homemade not "bacon" strips (recipe, p. 32)
- 1 Tbs. canola or olive oil
- 2 slices vegan bread per sandwich, toasted
- vegan mayonnaise as spread
- lettuce
- tomato slices
- *optional*:
  - avocado slices

TO PREPARE

Make homemade not "bacon" strips or sauté store-bought "bacon" in oil until crispy, stirring occasionally and drizzling with more oil as need to prevent sticking.

Place several pieces of "bacon" on a slice of toasted bread spread with mayonnaise. Add lettuce, tomato, and optional avocado, then cover with another piece of toasted bread, also spread with mayonnaise. Cut sandwich into 2 pieces.

Serve with french fries (recipe, p. 105), potato salad (recipe, p. 114), coleslaw (recipe, p. 115), or macaroni salad (recipe, 116).

CLUB SANDWICH

Makes 1

INGREDIENTS

- 2 Tbs. canola or olive oil
- 1 tsp. soy sauce
- 4 slices store-bought vegan turkey lunch meat or 3 slices no chicken seitan lunch meat (recipe, p. 34)
- 4 slices store-bought vegan "ham" or store-bought vegan "bacon" or 2 homemade not "bacon" strips (recipe, p. 32)
- yellow mustard as spread
- 3 slices vegan bread, toasted
- lettuce
- vegan mayonnaise as spread
- tomato slices
- *optional:*
    - avocado slices

TO PREPARE

Heat oil in a pan over medium heat.

Add vegan meats, one type at a time or segregated by type in pan while cooking. Drizzle with soy sauce and stir to coat. Cook until vegan meats are warmed through and slightly crispy, stirring occasionally and drizzling with more oil as need to prevent sticking.

Spread a small amount of mustard on one slice of toasted bread. Add vegan turkey or no chicken seitan slices, lettuce, and optional avocado.

Cover with second slice of toasted bread* spread with mayonnaise. Add "ham" or "bacon," and tomato slice.

Cover with third slice of toasted bread, spread with mayonnaise.

Cut sandwich into quarters. Place potato salad (recipe, p. 114) or french fries (recipe, p. 105) in the center of a plate, and surround with sandwich slices.

To hold the club, skip the center piece of bread.

PHILLY CHEESE STEAK SANDWICH

Makes 2

INGREDIENTS

- ½ cup sliced mushrooms
- ½ cup julienned yellow onion
- 2 Tbs. canola or olive oil
- 1 Tbs. minced garlic
- 5.5 oz. (1 package) store-bought vegan Philly cheese steak lunch meat or 8 no "beef" seitan lunch meat slices (recipe, p. 31) or 8 no chicken seitan lunch meat slices (recipe, p. 34)
- ½ cup julienned roasted red peppers*
- 1 tsp. soy sauce
- ¾ cup grated vegan cheese (any flavor)
- 1 vegan sandwich roll or 2 slices vegan bread per sandwich, toasted
- not so secret sauce as spread (recipe, p. 120)

Sold in jars at natural food stores.

TO PREPARE

In a pan, sauté mushrooms and onions in oil over medium heat until tender, then add garlic and sauté for 1 minute more.

Add vegan meat and red peppers, drizzle with soy sauce and stir to coat. Cook until vegan meats are warmed through and slightly crispy, stirring occasionally and drizzling with more oil as need to prevent sticking.

Sprinkle with cheese, cover pan, reduce heat to low and cook until cheese melts.

Stir and remove from heat.

Spread both slices of toasted bread with not so secret sauce. Heap one slice with seitan-pepper-cheese mixture, then cover with other slice. Cut sandwich into 2 pieces.

Serve with french fries (recipe, p. 105), potato salad (recipe, p. 114), coleslaw (recipe, p. 115), or macaroni salad (recipe, 116).

GRILLED CHEESE SANDWICH

Makes 1

INGREDIENTS

- 2 slices vegan white or sourdough bread
- vegan margarine as spread plus 1 Tbs. more for pan
- 1½ tsp. nutritional yeast, divided
- 4 Tbs. grated vegan cheddar cheese or 2 vegan cheese slices

TO PREPARE

Spread one slice of bread with margarine and sprinkle evenly with ½ tsp. nutritional yeast. Lay bread margarine side up on a plate.

Place cheese on top of this piece of bread.

Spread another piece of bread with margarine and place it on top of cheese, margarine side up. Sprinkle bread evenly with ½ tsp. nutritional yeast.

Microwave for 30-45 seconds to begin melting cheese.

Heat 1 Tbs. margarine in the center of a pan over medium heat.

When margarine is melted, sprinkle an area of the pan the size of the bread with ½ tsp. nutritional yeast and lay sandwich on top of this area, with the margarine side facing up (the plain side is the bottom of the sandwich). As bread will become hot from the microwave, use a spatula to handle it.

Sauté until bread touching pan is slightly crispy and golden brown, then flip and cook the other side until crispy and golden brown, too.

Cut sandwich into 2 pieces.

Note: Some vegan cheeses melt faster and better than others. While microwaving the sandwich first speeds this process, you may also want to cover the pan while cooking to direct heat back down into the sandwich.

REUBEN SANDWICH

Makes 2

INGREDIENTS

For Sandwich Filling
- 2 Tbs. canola or olive oil
- 1 cup julienned yellow onion
- pinch of salt
- 5.5 oz. (1 package) store-bought vegan turkey lunch meat slices or 8 no "beef" seitan lunch meat slices (recipe, p. 31) or 8 no chicken seitan lunch meat slices (recipe, p. 34)
- 1 tsp. soy sauce
- 1 cup grated vegan cheese (any flavor)

Also
- 2 slices vegan rye or pumpernickel bread per sandwich, toasted
- Thousand Island dressing as spread (recipe, p. 119)
- yellow mustard as spread
- 2-4 Tbs. drained vegan sauerkraut

TO PREPARE

To caramelize onions, heat oil in a pan over medium heat, then add onions. After a few minutes, sprinkle with a pinch of salt and reduce heat to medium-low. When onions start sticking to the pan, wait a few moments so the onions can brown, then stir them before they burn. Allow onions to stick and brown again, then stir, adding more oil as needed to prevent burning. Repeat this process until onions turn a deep golden brown.

Add vegan meat to pan. Drizzle with soy sauce and stir to coat. Cook until seitan slices are warmed through and slightly crispy, stirring occasionally and drizzling with more oil as needed to prevent sticking.

Sprinkle with cheese, cover pan, reduce heat to low and cook until cheese melts.

To Assemble: Spread one slice of toasted bread with Thousand Island dressing and the other slice of toasted bread with mustard.

Put 1-2 Tbs. sauerkraut on one slice of bread, then heap with seitan-onion mixture.

Place other slice of bread on top. Cut sandwich into 2 pieces.

Serve with french fries (recipe, p. 105), potato salad (recipe, p. 114), coleslaw (recipe, p. 115), or macaroni salad (recipe, 116).

NO TUNA FISH SANDWICH

Makes 4

INGREDIENTS

- 1 batch no tuna fish salad (recipe, p. 33)
- 2 slices vegan bread per sandwich
- *optional:*
  - avocado slices
  - lettuce

TO PREPARE

Place several scoops of no tuna fish salad on a slice of bread. Add optional avocado and lettuce, then cover with another piece of bread. Cut sandwich into 2 pieces.

For a TUNA MELT, follow the recipe for grilled cheese sandwich (recipe, p. 87), adding no tuna fish salad.

Serve with potato chips.

NO EGG SALAD SANDWICH

Makes 4

INGREDIENTS

- ⅔ cup vegan mayonnaise plus more as spread
- 1 Tbs. yellow mustard
- ¼ tsp. celery seed
- 2 Tbs. nutritional yeast
- ½ tsp. salt
- ¼ tsp. black pepper
- 2 cups pressed and crumbled firm tofu (see p. 35 for directions on how to press tofu)
- ⅓ cup diced celery
- 2 slices vegan bread per sandwich
- *optional:*
  - avocado slices
  - lettuce
  - tomato slices

TO PREPARE

Combine mayonnaise, mustard, celery seed, nutritional yeast, salt, and black pepper.

Add tofu and celery, stirring to combine.

Place several scoops of no egg salad on a slice of bread spread with vegan mayonnaise. Add optional avocado, lettuce, and tomato then cover with another piece of bread. Cut sandwich into 2 pieces.

Serve with potato chips.

SLOPPY JOES

Makes 4

INGREDIENTS

- 1 cup diced yellow onion
- 1 cup seeded and diced bell pepper
- 2 Tbs. canola or olive oil
- 2 cups store-bought vegan ground "beef" or shredded homemade no "beef" seitan cutlets (recipe, p. 31)
- 2 Tbs. garlic powder
- ½ tsp. chili powder
- 2 tsp. dried oregano
- 1 tsp. salt
- 8 oz. tomato sauce
- ¼ cup tomato paste
- 1 Tbs. yellow mustard
- 2 Tbs. maple syrup
- 1 vegan hamburger bun per sloppy joe

TO PREPARE

Sauté onion and bell pepper in oil until tender.

Add ground "beef," garlic powder, chili powder, oregano, salt, tomato sauce, and tomato paste.

Cook for 10 minutes over medium heat, stirring frequently.

Add mustard and maple syrup and stir to combine.

Serve on warmed hamburger buns with french fries (recipe, p. 105) or vegan tater tots.

Lunch & Dinner

WHY REINVENT THE WHEEL?

We've said it before, and we'll say it again: it is possible to make a delicious vegan version of every "food" Americans eat. And we wrote this cookbook to prove it. But we also wanted to show that vegan cooking can be just as easy and fast as traditional cooking, which is why we suggest you never make the following recipe. We stand by it, but we also think it is a waste of time given the number of great ready-made veggie burgers on the market today. The same is true of our french fry recipe. Try making a dinner that includes this hamburger recipe and fries from scratch, and you will shake your head in wonder that such a meal could ever be called "fast food." That said, if you love to cook, knock yourself out. But if you're like many Americans and would rather be doing something other than cooking, trade the two hours it takes to prepare this recipe for two minutes in the frozen food aisle, and get the same, tasty result.

HAMBURGER

Makes 6

INGREDIENTS

- 1½ cups plus 2 Tbs. hot vegan "beef" or vegetable broth
- 1 cup textured vegetable protein (TVP)*
- 1 cup sliced mushrooms
- ¼ cup diced yellow onion
- 2 Tbs. olive oil
- 2 tsp. minced garlic
- ½ tsp. liquid smoke hickory seasoning
- 2 Tbs. ketchup
- ½ tsp. marmite

- ¼ tsp. mustard powder
- 1 Tbs. vegan Worcestershire sauce
- ½ tsp. smoked paprika
- ⅛ tsp. chili powder
- ½ tsp. browning sauce
- 1½ cups wheat gluten flour
- ½ cup nutritional yeast

Textured Vegetable Protein is defatted soy flour in the form of small hard chunks. Look for it in the baking department of your natural food store.

TO PREPARE

In a large bowl, combine broth with TVP. Set aside.

In a pan, sauté mushrooms and onions in oil over medium heat until tender, then add garlic and sauté for 1 minute more.

continued...

Place onion-garlic-mushroom mixture in a food processor and shred into tiny pieces.

Separately, combine hickory seasoning, ketchup, marmite, mustard powder, Worcestershire sauce, smoked paprika, chili powder, and browning sauce. Combine these seasonings, the shredded onion-garlic-mushroom mixture, and the TVP-broth mixture.

Separately, combine gluten flour and nutritional yeast then add them to the TVP mixture, mixing to make a dough.

Shape dough into 6 hamburger-sized patties. Loosely wrap each individual patty in parchment paper, followed by aluminum foil.

Place patties in a steamer basket within a large stockpot containing water (filled to below the level of the patties) and cook for 1 hour, adding more water as needed to ensure a constant supply of steam.

When cool enough to handle, unwrap patties and sauté in oil or margarine before serving.

Serve on a toasted vegan hamburger bun with one or more of the following toppings: vegan cheese, grilled onions, lettuce, tomato, avocado, sautéed mushrooms, yellow mustard, ketchup, pickles, vegan relish, vegan mayonnaise, and/or not so secret sauce (recipe, p. 120). Add a side of french fries (recipe, p. 105).

BBQ NO RIBS

Makes 2 dozen

INGREDIENTS

- 1 lb. (2 packages) store-bought large chunk seitan or 4 homemade no chicken cutlets (recipe, p. 34) or no "beef" seitan cutlets (recipe, p. 31)
- 2½ cups store-bought or 1 batch homemade vegan BBQ sauce (recipe, p. 125)

TO PREPARE

Preheat oven to 350 degrees.

Cut seitan into ½ inch thick strips.

Dip strips in BBQ sauce until thoroughly coated and place on greased or parchment paper-lined baking sheet.

Bake for 20 minutes. If you want them well-done and a little crispy, cook another 5 minutes, broiling the last 2 minutes (monitor closely to avoid burning).

Serve with a side of coleslaw (recipe, p. 115), cornbread (recipe, p. 112), or vegan baked beans.

NO CHICKEN POT PIE

INGREDIENTS

Makes 1 pie

- 2 thawed, unbaked store-bought or homemade vegan pie crusts (recipe, p. 147)
- 1 cup vegan chicken broth
- ½ cup cashew cream (recipe, p. 39) or vegan non-dairy cream
- ¼ cup nutritional yeast
- ¼ cup all-purpose flour
- 1 tsp. garlic powder
- ¼ tsp. asafoetida
- ¼ tsp. salt
- ½ medium yellow onion, diced
- 3 Tbs. vegan margarine
- 8 oz. (1 package) store-bought chicken-style seitan strips or 1 cup (cut into ½ inch chunks) homemade no chicken seitan cutlets (recipe, p. 34)
- 1 cup frozen mixed vegetables (corn, peas, and carrots are a good blend)
- 1 large russet potato, baked or microwaved and cut into ½ inch chunks

TO PREPARE

Preheat oven to 375 degrees.

Blend broth, cream, nutritional yeast, flour, garlic powder, asafoetida, and salt together in a blender until smooth and free of lumps, then set aside.

Sauté onion in margarine in a pan until tender.

Add seitan, mixed vegetables, potatoes, and broth mixture to pan and, stirring occasionally, cook for a few minutes on medium-low heat until mixture thickens to a pudding-like consistency.

Place a pie crust onto a baking sheet (to protect oven from possible spillage when cooking).

Spoon or pour mixture into pie crust.

Cover pie with second crust (if store-bought, remove from pie pan and roll out to proper size), then seal crusts together and score top of pie with an X.

Bake for 25 minutes or until pie is golden brown.

Allow to cool 5 minutes before serving.

CORNDOGS

Makes 6

INGREDIENTS

- ¾ cup cornmeal
- 1¼ cups all-purpose flour
- 1 tsp. salt
- 4 Tbs. vegan sugar
- 1 tsp. baking powder
- reconstituted egg replacer powder equal to 2 eggs
- 1 cup plain unsweetened non-dairy milk

For Filling
- 6 store-bought vegan hot dogs or 6 homemade not sausages (recipe, p. 81)

Also
- canola oil for deep frying
- 6 skewers

TO PREPARE

In a large bowl, combine cornmeal, flour, salt, sugar, and baking powder.

Separately, combine egg replacer and non-dairy milk.

Prepare plate lined with paper towels to receive corndogs after frying to absorb excess oil.

Begin heating 3 inches of oil in a deep pot to 360 degrees.

While oil is heating, combine wet and dry ingredients, mixing to make a batter.

When oil reaches 360 degrees, fully submerge one hot dog or not sausage into the batter. Then slowly remove it, ensuring a thick coating.

Gently place corndog into hot oil. After a few seconds, gently flip using tongs or forks so it does not get bottom heavy. Continue frying, occasionally spinning or holding the corndog in place as needed to ensure an even golden brown.

When done, remove to paper towels. Repeat with remaining hot dogs or not sausages.

When cool enough to handle, insert a skewer into the bottom center of each corndog before serving.

Serve with ketchup and/or yellow mustard.

FRIED NO CHICKEN

Serves 4

INGREDIENTS

For Batter
- ¾ cup all-purpose flour
- 1 tsp. baking powder
- ½ tsp. salt
- 1½ tsp. egg replacer powder
- 1 cup cashew cream (recipe, p. 39) or vegan non-dairy cream
- 1 tsp. canola or olive oil
- 4 Tbs. water

For Seasoning
- 1 cup all-purpose flour
- 1 tsp. salt
- ½ tsp. vegan sugar
- 1 tsp. black pepper
- 1 tsp. chili powder
- 1 tsp. dried ground sage
- 1 tsp. dried basil
- 1 tsp. dried marjoram
- 1 tsp. paprika
- 1 tsp. onion powder
- 1 tsp. garlic powder
- 4 Tbs. nutritional yeast

Also
- 1 lb. (2 packages) store-bought large chunk chicken-style seitan or 4 home-made no chicken seitan cutlets (recipe, p. 34)
- canola oil for deep frying

TO PREPARE

Batter: Mix all batter ingredients in a bowl and pour into a shallow dish. Batter should be thick, but liquid enough to cling to seitan cutlets when dipped in. Add small, additional amounts of cream if needed to reach this desired consistency.

Seasoning: Separately, mix all seasoning ingredients in a shallow dish.

Prepare plate lined with paper towels to receive seitan after frying to absorb excess oil.

Dip seitan chunks or cutlets in batter, then seasoning, coating thoroughly with both. Place pieces on a plate without overlapping to await frying.

Heat 2 inches of oil in a deep pot to 360 degrees.

Place seitan pieces (in manageable amounts) in oil for 1-2 minutes until golden brown, flipping pieces as needed to ensure even cooking. Remove to paper towels.

Serve with mashed potatoes (recipe, p. 109), gravy (recipe, p. 124), buttermilk biscuits (recipe, p. 111), and sweet corn.

To make NO CHICKEN FINGERS, cut seitan into strips before battering and frying, then serve with Ranch dip (recipe, p. 118), tartar sauce (recipe, p. 121), or warmed BBQ sauce (recipe, p. 125).

MACARONI & CHEESE

Serves 4

INGREDIENTS

- 1 lb. uncooked vegan macaroni
- ¼ cup vegan margarine
- ⅛ cup vegan cream cheese
- 1 cup vegan non-dairy cream
- 2 cups grated vegan cheddar cheese
- ¾ cup nutritional yeast
- ⅛ tsp. salt
- *optional:*
  - 1½ tsp. umeboshi plum vinegar (for extra tang)

TO PREPARE

Cook macaroni al dente according to package directions. Do not overcook.

While macaroni is cooking, combine margarine, cream cheese, and cream in a pot over medium heat, stirring occasionally.

After margarine and cream cheese have melted, add grated cheese, stirring occasionally until melted. Cover pot between stirrings to speed the melting.

Stir in nutritional yeast, salt, and optional vinegar.

After macaroni is cooked and drained, combine with cheese sauce, stirring to coat.

Serve as a main dish or as a side with sandwiches.

PIZZA

Makes 1 pizza

INGREDIENTS

For Crust
- 2 tsp. (1 packet) active dry yeast
- 1 tsp. vegan sugar
- ¾ cup warm water
- 1 tsp. salt
- 2 cups all-purpose flour
- ½ cup oat flour
- 1 Tbs. olive oil

For Pizza Sauce
- ¾ cup tomato sauce
- 2 Tbs. nutritional yeast
- ½ tsp. minced garlic
- ½ tsp. dried basil
- ½ tsp. onion powder
- ¼ tsp. salt

For Toppings
- yellow cornmeal for dusting pan
- 2 Tbs. olive oil, divided
- 1½ cups grated vegan mozzarella cheese
- 1 Tbs. store-bought or homemade vegan parmesan (recipe, p. 126)
- 2 Tbs. nutritional yeast
- salt to taste
- *optional:*
  - sautéed store-bought vegan pepperoni
  - sautéed sliced not sausages (recipe, p. 81)
  - sautéed mushrooms
  - caramelized onions

TO PREPARE

Crust: In a large bowl, dissolve yeast and 1 tsp. sugar in warm water and let stand for 5-10 minutes to proof (yeast should foam).

Separately, combine salt, all-purpose flour, and oat flour.

Combine salt-flour mixture, oil, and dissolved yeast mixture, mixing to make a dough.

Turn dough out onto a lightly floured surface, and knead for 5 minutes, dusting with more flour as needed to prevent sticking.

Place dough in a well-greased bowl, flip, and cover with a damp kitchen towel or plastic wrap. Let rise for 1 hour.

Sauce: While dough is rising, combine all sauce ingredients in a small saucepan. Bring to a boil, then reduce heat to simmer and cook for 3 minutes, stirring occasionally. Remove from heat and set aside, allowing to cool before use or yeast in pizza dough could deactivate.

After dough has risen, preheat oven to 450 degrees.

Punch dough down and roll out onto a lightly floured surface to ¼ thick and shaped to fit your pan.

Dust pan lightly with cornmeal, then place dough on top.

Drizzle crust with approximately 1 Tbs. olive oil and spread evenly with a spatula or the back of a spoon.

Cover pizza with sauce, ⅛ inch thick to within ½ inch of edge.

continued...

Sprinkle pizza evenly with cheese, then vegan parmesan, nutritional yeast, and any optional toppings. Drizzle with 1 Tbs. olive oil and sprinkle with salt.

Bake for 10-15 minutes until cheese is melted and crust is lightly browned. Then broil for 1 minute to thoroughly melt cheese (monitor closely to avoid burning).

Allow to cool slightly before cutting into wedges for serving.

LASAGNA

Serves 10

INGREDIENTS

- 1½ lbs. (1½ packages) uncooked vegan lasagna noodles

For Tofu Ricotta Filling
- 8 oz. crumbled firm tofu
- 2 tsp. nutritional yeast
- ½ tsp. onion powder
- 1½ Tbs. lemon juice
- ¼ cup cashew cream (recipe, p. 39)
- 1½ tsp. white miso
- ½ tsp. salt
- ⅛ tsp. black pepper

For Vegan Meat Filling
- ½ medium yellow onion, diced
- 24 oz. (2 packages) store-bought vegan ground "beef" or 3 homemade no "beef" cutlets (recipe, p. 31), shredded
- 2 Tbs. olive oil

Also
- olive oil for greasing dish and drizzling
- 31 oz. (1¼ jars) store-bought vegan spaghetti sauce

- 1½ cups grated vegan cheese
- 1 bag frozen spinach, thawed and squeezed out to reduce moisture or 3 cups fresh spinach, chopped
- 1 tsp. garlic powder, divided
- 6 Tbs. store-bought or homemade vegan parmesan (recipe, p. 126), divided
- 6 Tbs. nutritional yeast, divided
- ¾ tsp. salt, divided

TO PREPARE

Noodles: Prepare noodles according to package directions, then cover with cold water to prevent sticking. Set aside.

Tofu Ricotta: Blend all ingredients in a food processor until the texture of ricotta. Adjust salt to taste.

Vegan Meat Filling: Sauté onion and vegan "beef" in oil until onions are tender and vegan "beef" is slightly crispy.

Preheat oven to 375 degrees.

Grease the bottom of a large baking dish with olive oil.

Pour ¼ jar spaghetti sauce in dish, and spread evenly.

continued...

Spread one layer of thoroughly drained noodles evenly in pan and spread another ¼ jar of sauce evenly over them.

Spread half of the following ingredients evenly over noodles, one atop the other, in the following order: ricotta (this may have to be applied in small dollops), vegan meat-onion mixture, vegan cheese, and spinach. Then sprinkle evenly with ½ tsp. garlic powder, 2 Tbs. vegan parmesan, 2 Tbs. nutritional yeast, and ¼ tsp. salt. Drizzle lightly with olive oil.

Spread evenly with another layer of noodles and another ¼ jar of spaghetti sauce. Repeat the previous step.

Cover with one last layer of noodles.

Pour ¼ jar spaghetti sauce on top layer or more as needed to thoroughly coat noodles. Sprinkle evenly with 2 Tbs. vegan parmesan, 2 Tbs. nutritional yeast, and ¼ tsp. salt. Drizzle lightly with olive oil.

Cover with parchment paper, then foil.

Bake for 40 minutes, until lasagna bubbles.

Remove covering and bake for an additional 5 minutes. Then broil for 2 minutes to brown (monitor closely to avoid burning).

Serve with garlic bread (recipe, p. 108) and Caesar salad (recipe, p. 117).

SIDES

Sides

NO CHICKEN NOODLE SOUP

Serves 4

INGREDIENTS

- 3 oz. uncooked vegan fettuccine, broken into thirds
- 2 carrots, sliced ⅛ inch thick
- 3 celery stalks, sliced ⅛ inch thick
- 1 cup diced yellow onion
- 3 Tbs. vegan margarine
- 6 cups vegan chicken broth
- 1 cup cashew cream (recipe, p. 39)
- 1 bay leaf
- 8 oz. (1 package) store-bought vegan chicken-style seitan or 2 homemade no chicken seitan cutlets (recipe, p. 34), cut into ¼ inch chunks

TO PREPARE

Cook fettuccine al dente according to package directions. Do not overcook.

In a large stockpot, sauté carrots, celery, and onions in margarine until tender.

Add broth and cashew cream and bring to a boil.

Reduce heat to low and add bay leaf and seitan. Simmer for 10 minutes.

Add drained fettuccine.

Serve with vegan crackers, buttermilk biscuits (recipe, p. 111), or crescent rolls (recipe, p. 155).

CREAM OF MUSHROOM SOUP

Serves 4

INGREDIENTS

- 8 oz. sliced mushrooms
- ½ cup diced yellow onion
- 1 bay leaf
- ⅛ tsp. dried thyme
- 4 Tbs. vegan margarine, divided
- 2½ cups vegan chicken or vegetable broth
- 2 Tbs. all-purpose flour
- 2 cups cashew cream (recipe, p. 39)

TO PREPARE

In a large stockpot, sauté mushrooms, onions, bay leaf, and thyme in 3 Tbs. margarine over medium heat until mushrooms and onions are tender.

Add broth, bring to a boil and simmer 5 minutes. Remove bay leaf.

Puree this mixture with flour in a blender, leaving a few chunks. Be careful when blending hot liquid, as it can push the lid off of the blender. Place lid on tight, cover with dish towel and hold lid down tightly before turning the blender on.

Melt 1 Tbs. margarine in empty stockpot, then whisk in flour, stirring until smooth.

Return mushroom puree to stockpot, then add cream.

Stirring constantly, bring to a boil. Soup should be the consistency of cream soup. If not, reduce heat to simmer and cook a few minutes more.

Serve with vegan crackers, buttermilk biscuits (recipe, p. 111), or crescent rolls (recipe, p. 155).

Sides

MATZO BALL SOUP

Serves 4

INGREDIENTS

For Matzo Balls
- 1½ cups vegan matzo meal (*not* matzo ball mix)
- 1¾ tsp. salt, divided
- ¾ tsp. black pepper
- 1½ cups (1 package) firm silken tofu
- ½ cup vegan chicken or vegetable broth
- ¼ cup olive oil

For Broth
- 1 cup diced yellow onion
- 2 Tbs. vegan margarine or olive oil
- 2 tsp. minced garlic
- 8 cups vegan chicken or vegetable broth
- 1 bay leaf
- 1 tsp. dill
- 1 tsp. parsley

TO PREPARE

Matzo balls: In a large bowl, combine matzo meal, ¾ tsp. salt, and black pepper.

In a blender or food processor, combine tofu, broth, and oil until smooth.

Combine wet and dry ingredients, mixing to make a dough.

Cover matzo ball mixture with plastic wrap and refrigerate for 1 hour.

When matzo ball mixture is thoroughly chilled, fill a large stockpot with water and 1 tsp. salt and bring to a boil.

Form matzo ball mixture into 1 inch balls and gently place in water. Reduce heat to medium-low and cook matzo balls for 30 minutes.

Broth: 20 minutes before matzo balls are ready, sauté onion in margarine or oil over medium heat until tender. Add garlic and sauté for one minute more.

Add broth and bay leaf and bring to a boil. Then add dill and parsley and reduce to simmer.

When matzo balls are done cooking in salt water, gently remove with a slotted spoon or skimmer and place in broth.

Serve with vegan crackers, buttermilk biscuits (recipe, p. 111), or crescent rolls (recipe, p. 155).

FRENCH FRIES

Serves 4

INGREDIENTS

- 4 large russet potatoes, peeled and cut into french fry-sized sticks
- canola or peanut oil for deep frying
- salt and black pepper to taste

TO PREPARE

Place peeled and cut potatoes in ice water and chill for at least 1 hour.

Drain and blot potatoes dry.

Heat 2 inches of oil in a deep pot to 325 degrees.

Prepare plate lined with paper towels to receive fries after cooking to absorb excess oil.

Working in batches, add potatoes to oil, stirring occasionally until potatoes turn slightly opaque, about 7 minutes.

Using a skimmer or a slotted spoon, remove and place on paper towels.

Let fries cool for approximately 10 minutes.

Prepare a new plate lined with paper towels.

Heat oil to 375 degrees.

Working in batches, re-fry the potatoes for about 4 minutes until they are crispy.

Remove and place on paper towels.

Season to taste with salt and pepper.

Serve hot with a hamburger (recipe, p. 92) or club sandwich (recipe, p. 85).

Sides

ONION RINGS

Serves 4

INGREDIENTS

- 2 small yellow onions or 1 large Vidalia onion, peeled and cut into ½ inch wide rings and separated individually
- 2 cups all-purpose flour
- 1 Tbs. vegan brown sugar
- 1 tsp. salt plus more to taste
- 1 tsp. baking powder
- canola oil for deep frying
- 1½ cups vegan beer*

*Beer, wine, and other alcoholic beverages are often made using animal-derived ingredients. Go to allamericanvegan.com for a list of vegan-friendly beers, wines, and spirits.

TO PREPARE

In a large bowl, combine flour, brown sugar, salt, and baking powder.

Prepare plate lined with paper towels to receive onion rings after frying to absorb excess oil.

Heat 2 inches of oil in a deep pot to 360 degrees.

While oil is heating, add beer to dry mixture and mix until the consistency of pancake batter, liquid enough to cling evenly to onions when dipped in. Add small, additional amounts of beer if needed to reach the desired consistency.

Dip peeled and cut rings in batter, and then place gently into oil. Be prepared, they will cook very quickly.

When lightly browned on one side, flip using fork or tongs and cook other side. Using a skimmer or a slotted spoon, remove and place on paper towels.

Sprinkle with salt.

Serve hot with ketchup or not so secret sauce (recipe, p. 120).

MOZZARELLA STICKS

Serves 4

INGREDIENTS

- ¾ cup Italian-style dried vegan bread-crumbs
- ¼ cup store-bought or homemade vegan parmesan (recipe, p. 126)
- ¼ cup nutritional yeast
- ¼ tsp. salt
- 1 cup cashew cream (recipe, p. 39)
- 8 oz. block vegan mozzarella, cut into sticks 4 inches long x ½ inch wide x ½ inch thick
- canola oil for deep frying

TO PREPARE

In a shallow dish, combine bread crumbs, parmesan, nutritional yeast, and salt.

Separately, pour cashew cream in a shallow dish.

Dip cheese sticks in cashew cream, then roll in crumbs, coating thoroughly. Repeat.

Place sticks on a plate and then in the freezer for at least 1 hour.

Prepare plate lined with paper towels to receive mozzarella sticks after frying to absorb excess oil.

Heat 2 inches of oil in a deep pot to 360 degrees.

Place sticks in oil. Be prepared, they will cook very quickly.

When lightly browned on one side, flip using fork or tongs and cook other side. Using a skimmer or a slotted spoon, remove and place on paper towels.

Serve hot with warm vegan spaghetti sauce for dipping.

Sides

GARLIC BREAD

Serves 4

INGREDIENTS

- 1 loaf vegan Italian or French bread (unsliced)
- ½ cup vegan margarine, softened
- 2 Tbs. garlic powder or 4 tsp. fresh minced garlic
- ¼ cup nutritional yeast
- 1 Tbs. chopped parsley (fresh or dry)
- 1 Tbs. store-bought or homemade vegan parmesan (recipe, p. 126)

TO PREPARE

Cut the bread in half, horizontally.

Combine margarine, garlic, nutritional yeast, parsley and parmesan, making a paste.

Spread mixture evenly over the two bread halves.

Place on a baking pan, margarine side up, and bake for 10 minutes.

Move bread to highest oven rack and set oven to broil.

Broil for 1-2 minutes until the edges of the bread begin to toast and the topping begins to bubble (monitor closely to avoid burning).

When cool enough to handle, cut into 1 inch thick slices.

Serve with lasagna (recipe, p. 99).

MASHED POTATOES

Serves 4

INGREDIENTS

- 5 large russet potatoes, peeled and cut into 1 inch chunks
- 2 tsp. salt, divided plus more to taste
- ½ cup cashew cream (recipe, p. 39) or vegan non-dairy cream
- 5 Tbs. vegan margarine
- black pepper to taste

TO PREPARE

Place potato chunks in a large pot and cover with water.

Add 1 tsp. salt.

Bring to a boil over high heat, then reduce heat to medium-low. Cook until tender, about 15-20 minutes.

Separately, heat cream in saucepan over low heat while potatoes are boiling.

Drain potatoes then return to pot, off of stove.

Mash potatoes with a masher, a potato ricer, or a mixer.

Add margarine, 1 tsp. salt, and pepper and mix.

Gradually add in heated cream to achieve potatoes that are smooth, moist, light, and fluffy. Do not overwork.

Adjust salt to taste.

Serve with fried no chicken (recipe, p. 96) and gravy (recipe, p. 124) or stuffed not a turkey with maple glazed root vegetables (recipe, p. 152).

Sides

BUFFALO STRIPS

Serves 4

INGREDIENTS

- ¾ cup all-purpose flour
- 1 tsp. garlic powder
- 1 tsp. cayenne pepper
- 2 Tbs. nutritional yeast
- 1 tsp. salt
- 1½ cups (1½ packages) store-bought seitan or 3 homemade no chicken seitan cutlets (recipe, p. 34) or no "beef" seitan cutlets (recipe, p. 31), cut into strips 4 inches long x 1 inch wide x ¼ inch thick

For Sauce
- ½ cup vegan margarine
- ½ cup vegan hot sauce
- 1 tsp. balsamic vinegar
- 4 Tbs. maple syrup

TO PREPARE

Preheat oven to 400 degrees.

In a plastic freezer bag, combine flour, garlic powder, cayenne pepper, nutritional yeast, and salt.

Pat seitan dry, then place in bag and shake to coat.

Sauce: In a small saucepan over low heat, combine margarine, hot sauce, vinegar, and maple syrup, stirring constantly. When margarine is thoroughly melted, remove from heat.

Individually, remove strips from bag and using a fork or tongs, dip each strip in saucepan until it is thoroughly coated. Remove to a greased or parchment paper-lined baking sheet.

Bake strips until golden brown, about 15 minutes.

Serve strips with Ranch dip (recipe, p. 118).

BUTTERMILK BISCUITS

Makes 9

INGREDIENTS

- 1 tsp. lemon juice
- ⅔ cup vegan non-dairy cream
- 2 cups all-purpose flour
- 2 tsp. vegan sugar
- 2 tsp. baking powder
- ½ tsp. baking soda
- 1 tsp. salt
- ⅓ cup vegan margarine

TO PREPARE

Preheat oven to 450 degrees.

Combine lemon juice with cream to make "buttermilk." Set aside.

In a large bowl, combine flour, sugar, baking powder, baking soda, and salt.

Cut margarine into flour mixture until it resembles coarse meal.

Combine wet and dry ingredients, mixing to make a fluffy and slightly sticky dough. Do not overwork.

Roll out dough on a lightly floured surface to ½ inch thick.

Cut out biscuits using a 2 inch biscuit cutter or a straight-edged drinking glass.

Place on ungreased baking sheet.

Bake 7-8 minutes until golden brown on top and fully cooked in the center. Open one biscuit to make sure it is fully cooked throughout. If not, bake for an additional 1-2 minutes.

Serve warm with vegan jam or margarine, whipped sweet butter (recipe, p. 123), or gravy (recipe, p. 124).

Sides

CORNBREAD

Serves 6

INGREDIENTS

- 1 cup all-purpose flour
- 1 cup yellow cornmeal
- ½ cup vegan sugar
- ½ tsp. salt
- 3½ tsp. baking powder
- reconstituted egg replacer powder equal to 1 egg
- 1 cup non-dairy milk
- ½ cup canola oil

TO PREPARE

Preheat oven to 400 degrees.

Grease an 8 x 8 inch square pan.

In a large bowl, combine all ingredients, mixing to make a batter.

Pour batter into prepared pan.

Bake for 15-20 minutes, or until a toothpick inserted into the center of the loaf comes out clean.

Serve with whipped sweet butter (recipe, p. 123), BBQ no ribs (recipe, p. 93), and coleslaw (recipe, p. 115).

NACHOS

Serves 4

INGREDIENTS

- 1 can (16 oz.) black or pinto or vege-tarian refried beans
- 1 small yellow onion, diced
- 12 oz. (1 package) store-bought vegan ground "beef" or 2 homemade no "beef" seitan cutlets (recipe, p. 31), shredded
- 2 Tbs. canola or olive oil
- 1 lb. (1 bag) plain tortilla chips
- 2 cups grated nacho or cheddar vegan cheese
- 1 cup vegan guacamole
- 1 cup vegan sour cream
- 1 cup vegan salsa

TO PREPARE

Preheat oven to 350 degrees.

Heat beans in a saucepan until warmed through.

In a separate pan, sauté onion and vegan "beef" in oil over medium heat until onions are tender and vegan "beef" is slightly crispy.

Spread tortilla chips evenly in a large baking dish. Add the following ingredients evenly, one layer at a time, in the following order: beans (if using refried, you will have to spread in small dollops), ground "beef"-onion mixture, cheese.

Bake for 5 minutes, then broil for 1-2 minutes until cheese melts (monitor closely to avoid burning).

Add the remaining ingredients evenly, one layer at a time, in the following order: guacamole, sour cream (stir vigorously in tub before spreading so it is thinner, adding 1 Tbs. water to di-lute if needed), salsa.

Serve immediately.

Sides

POTATO SALAD

Serves 4

INGREDIENTS

- 5 medium russet potatoes
- 1 cup vegan mayonnaise
- ⅓ cup vegan sweet pickle relish or minced vegan dill pickles
- 2 Tbs. yellow mustard
- 1 tsp. dill weed
- ¼ tsp. black pepper
- ¼ tsp. paprika
- ¼ tsp. celery seed
- ¾ tsp. salt plus more to taste
- ½ cup diced red onion

TO PREPARE

Submerge potatoes in a large pot of water. Bring to a boil over high heat, then reduce heat to medium-low, cover, and boil until tender. Begin checking for tenderness after 25 minutes. Do not overcook.

Drain and refrigerate potatoes until cold.

Peel and cube potatoes.

In a large bowl, combine mayonnaise, relish or pickles, mustard, dill, black pepper, paprika, celery seed, and salt.

Add onion and potatoes. Stir to coat. Adjust salt to taste.

For best taste, refrigerate several hours or overnight before serving, re-seasoning as needed.

Serve as a side with sandwiches.

COLESLAW

Serves 6

INGREDIENTS

- 2 Tbs. lemon juice
- 1 Tbs. white vinegar
- ½ cup cashew cream (recipe, p. 39) or vegan non-dairy cream
- ½ cup vegan mayonnaise
- ⅓ cup vegan sugar
- 1 tsp. salt
- ⅛ tsp. black pepper
- 1 tsp. dill weed
- 4 Tbs. diced red onions
- 8 cups (1 head) shredded cabbage
- ¼ cup shredded carrot

TO PREPARE

Mix lemon juice, vinegar, and cream. Let stand for 5 minutes.

Combine cream mixture, mayonnaise, sugar, salt, pepper, and dill.

Add onions, cabbage, and carrots. Stir to coat.

For best taste, refrigerate several hours or overnight before serving, re-seasoning as needed.

Serve with BBQ no ribs (recipe, p. 93) and cornbread (recipe, p. 112) or fried no chicken (recipe, p. 96) and buttermilk biscuits (recipe, p. 111).

Sides

MACARONI SALAD

Serves 4

INGREDIENTS

- 8 oz. uncooked vegan macaroni
- 1½ cups vegan mayonnaise
- 2 Tbs. lemon juice
- 1 Tbs. vegan sugar
- ¼ cup diced vegan dill pickles
- ¼ cup diced carrots
- ¼ cup diced black or green olives
- ⅓ cup diced red onion
- ¼ cup diced celery
- 1 Tbs. minced fresh parsley
- ⅛ tsp. celery seed
- 1 tsp. dill weed
- ¼ tsp. garlic powder
- ⅛ tsp. black pepper
- ¼ tsp. salt plus more to taste

TO PREPARE

Cook macaroni al dente according to package directions. Do not overcook.

Separately, combine remaining ingredients.

Add macaroni and stir to coat. Adjust salt to taste.

For best taste, refrigerate several hours or overnight before serving, re-seasoning as needed.

Serve as a side with sandwiches.

CAESAR SALAD DRESSING

Makes ⅔ cup

INGREDIENTS

- ½ cup vegan mayonnaise
- ¼ cup cashew cream (recipe, p. 39)
- 2 Tbs. white miso
- 2 Tbs. lemon juice
- 1 garlic clove, minced
- 1 tsp. capers, drained
- 1 Tbs. store-bought vegan parmesan
- ¼ tsp. black pepper
- ⅛ tsp. salt
- *optional:*
    -1 inch x 1 inch square of dried nori
    (to replace anchovies)

TO PREPARE

Puree ingredients together in food processor or blender, adjusting salt to taste.

Toss with torn Romaine lettuce.

Sides

RANCH DIP & DRESSING

Makes ½ cup dip
Makes ¾ cup dressing

INGREDIENTS

For Dip
- ⅓ cup vegan mayonnaise
- ¼ cup vegan sour cream
- 5 Tbs. vegan cream cheese
- 2 Tbs. minced green onion
- 1 Tbs. minced fresh parsley
- 1 tsp. apple cider vinegar
- 1 tsp. yellow mustard
- ½ tsp. garlic powder
- ¼ tsp. black pepper
- ½ tsp. dill weed
- 1 tsp. lemon juice
- ¼ tsp. salt

For Dressing
- all of the above ingredients
- ¼ cup cashew cream (recipe, p. 39)
  or vegan non-dairy cream

TO PREPARE DIP

Blend all ingredients until smooth.

Serve with potato chips, vegan crackers, or cut vegetables.

TO PREPARE DRESSING

Blend all ingredients until smooth. Adjust salt to taste.

Toss with chopped lettuce.

THOUSAND ISLAND DRESSING

Makes 1⅔ cups

INGREDIENTS

- ½ cup firm silken tofu
- ½ cup vegan mayonnaise
- ⅓ cup ketchup
- 2 Tbs. maple syrup
- 2 Tbs. cashew cream (recipe, p. 39)
- ½ tsp. black pepper
- ½ cup chopped vegan dill pickles

TO PREPARE

Combine all ingredients except pickles in a food processor until smooth.

Add pickles and pulse until pickles are minced.

Toss with chopped lettuce or use as sandwich spread.

Sides

NOT SO SECRET SAUCE

Makes ¾ cup

INGREDIENTS

- ½ cup vegan mayonnaise
- ¼ cup ketchup
- ½ tsp. garlic powder
- ¼ tsp. vegan Worcestershire sauce
- ¼ tsp. black pepper
- 2 Tbs. vegan sweet relish

TO PREPARE

Combine all ingredients and stir until smooth.

Serve as spread on sandwiches or hamburgers (recipe, p. 92).

TARTAR SAUCE

Makes 1 cup

INGREDIENTS

- 1 cup vegan mayonnaise
- 1 Tbs. vegan sweet pickle relish
- 1 Tbs. minced white onion
- 2 Tbs. lemon juice
- salt and black pepper to taste

TO PREPARE

Combine mayonnaise, relish, onion, and lemon juice and stir until smooth.

Season to taste with salt and pepper.

Serve with no chicken fingers (recipe, p. 96).

WARMED FRUIT TOPPING

Makes 1 cup

INGREDIENTS

- 1 cup diced fruit (bananas, peaches, strawberries, pears, and/or plums)
- 2 Tbs. vegan margarine
- 1 Tbs. maple syrup

TO PREPARE

Sauté fruit over medium heat in margarine and maple syrup until the fruit is soft, about 4 minutes.

Serve warm over pancakes (recipe, p. 80), french toast (recipe, p. 78), ice cream (recipes, pp. 142-144), or cheesecake (recipe, p. 138).

WHIPPED SWEET BUTTER

Makes ½ cup

INGREDIENTS

- ½ cup vegan margarine
- ¼ cup vegan powdered sugar

TO PREPARE

Whip ingredients together with a mixer until smooth and fluffy, stopping several times to scrape the sides of the bowl.

Serve with vegan toast, pancakes (recipe, p. 80), french toast (recipe, p. 78), buttermilk biscuits (recipe, p. 111), banana nut bread (recipe, p. 73), or blueberry muffins (recipe, p. 71).

Sides

GRAVY

Makes 2 cups

INGREDIENTS

- ⅓ cup olive oil
- ½ cup minced yellow onion
- 1 tsp. minced garlic
- ½ tsp. dried thyme
- ½ tsp. dried ground sage
- ⅓ cup all-purpose flour
- 2 cups vegan broth (any flavor)
- 1 tsp. vegan Worcestershire sauce
- 1 tsp. soy sauce
- 1 Tbs. nutritional yeast
- 1 tsp. dried parsley
- ⅛ tsp. salt
- ⅛ tsp. black pepper

TO PREPARE

Heat oil in small saucepan over medium heat. Add onion and cook until tender. Then add garlic, thyme, and sage and cook for 1 minute more.

Reduce heat to low, whisk in flour, and cook for 2 minutes.

Slowly add the 2 cups of broth, whisking to combine.

Add remaining ingredients and cook, stirring constantly, until thickened, a few minutes more.

Serve with mashed potatoes (recipe, p. 109), buttermilk biscuits (recipe, p. 111), no chicken pot pie (recipe, p. 94), or stuffed not a turkey with maple glazed root vegetables (recipe, p. 152).

Makes 2½ cups

INGREDIENTS

- ¼ cup minced yellow onion
- 2 Tbs. olive oil
- 1½ tsp. minced garlic
- 2 cups ketchup
- ½ cup molasses
- ¼ tsp. cayenne pepper
- 1 Tbs. liquid smoke hickory seasoning
- 1½ tsp. vegan Worcestershire sauce

TO PREPARE

Sauté onions in oil over medium heat until tender, then add garlic and sauté for 1 minute more.

Puree remaining ingredients and onion-garlic mixture in food processor or blender until smooth.

Use to prepare BBQ no ribs (recipe, p. 93) or warm and use as a dipping sauce for no chicken fingers (recipe, p. 96).

★ ★ ★

PARMESAN

Makes 1¼ cups

INGREDIENTS

- 1 cup raw walnuts
- ¾ cup nutritional yeast
- 1 tsp. salt
- ½ tsp. onion powder
- ½ tsp. garlic powder

TO PREPARE

Combine all ingredients in a food processor until the texture of parmesan cheese.

Use to prepare garlic bread (recipe, p. 108), pizza (recipe, p. 98), or sprinkle on pasta or popcorn.

Store in refrigerator.

★★★

DESSERTS

Desserts

APPLE PIE

Makes 1 pie

INGREDIENTS

- 2 unbaked store-bought or homemade made vegan pie crusts (recipe, p. 147)

For Filling
- 5 cups cored, peeled, and sliced tart apples, such as Northern Spy, Granny Smith, or Jonathan
- 3 Tbs. maple syrup
- 1 tsp. lemon juice
- 1 Tbs. all-purpose flour
- ¼ tsp. grated nutmeg
- 1 tsp. ground cinnamon

TO PREPARE

Preheat oven to 350 degrees.

Filling: In a large bowl, combine apple chunks, maple syrup, and lemon juice.

Sprinkle with flour, nutmeg, and cinnamon. Stir to coat.

Pour apple mixture into pie crust, spreading evenly throughout.

Cover pie with second crust (if store-bought, remove from pie pan and roll out to proper size), then seal crusts together and score top of pie with an X.

Bake 45-50 minutes or until apples are tender, crust is golden brown, and juice begins to bubble. If edges begin to over-brown before pie is finished, cover with a 2-3 inch strip of aluminum foil or a pie edge protector.

Serve à la mode with vanilla ice cream (recipe, p. 142).

CHERRY PIE

Makes 1 pie

INGREDIENTS

- 2 unbaked store-bought or homemade vegan pie crusts (recipe, p. 147)

For Filling
- 1 cup vegan sugar
- ⅓ cup all-purpose flour
- 4 cups pitted tart cherries (fresh or frozen)
- 2 Tbs. vegan margarine, divided into several dollops

TO PREPARE

Preheat oven to 350 degrees.

Filling: In a large bowl, combine sugar and flour, then stir in cherries.

Pour cherry mixture into pie crust, spreading evenly through-out.

Drop several even-sized dollops of margarine throughout cherry mixture.

Cover pie with second crust (if store-bought, remove from pie pan and roll out to proper size), then seal crusts together and score top of pie with an X. Alternatively, cut second pie crust into ¾ inch wide strips, and use them to create a lattice pattern across the top of the pie. Seal top strips and bottom crust together.

Bake 45-50 minutes or until cherries are tender, crust is golden brown, and juice begins to bubble. If edges begin to overbrown before pie is finished, cover with a 2-3 inch strip of aluminum foil or a pie edge protector.

Desserts

BANANA CREAM PIE

Makes 1 pie

INGREDIENTS

- 1 prebaked store-bought or home-made vegan pie crust (recipe, p. 147)
- 1 batch coconut whipped topping (recipe, p. 148)

For Filling
- 1½ cups (1 package) firm silken tofu
- ¾ cup vegan sugar
- 2 Tbs. cornstarch
- ¼ tsp. salt
- 4 bananas (2 mashed and the other 2 cut into ¼ inch slices)

TO PREPARE

Make coconut whipped topping and store in refrigerator until needed.

Filling: Combine tofu, sugar, cornstarch, salt, and 2 mashed bananas in a blender or food processor until smooth.

Line the bottom of a prebaked but cooled pie crust with the banana slices, so they are touching but not overlapping.

Pour filling on top of bananas, spreading evenly throughout.

Distribute coconut whipped topping evenly over pie.

Refrigerate until thoroughly chilled and set, at least 5 hours but preferably overnight.

Serve drizzled with chocolate sauce (recipe, p. 146).

Store pie in refrigerator.

COCONUT CREAM PIE

Makes 1 pie

INGREDIENTS

- 1 prebaked store-bought or home-made vegan pie crust (recipe, p. 147)
- 1 batch coconut whipped topping (recipe, p. 148)

For Filling
- 1½ cups (1 package) firm silken tofu
- ¾ cup vegan sugar
- 5 Tbs. cornstarch
- 13 oz. (1 can) coconut milk (regular, not light)
- ¼ tsp. salt
- ¼ tsp. vanilla
- ½ cup shredded coconut

For Topping
- ½ cup shredded coconut
- 2 Tbs. vegan powdered sugar

TO PREPARE

Make coconut whipped topping and store in refrigerator until needed.

Filling: Blend tofu in blender or food processor until smooth.

In a saucepan off of stove, whisk together sugar and cornstarch. Add coconut milk and salt, whisking to combine. Stirring constantly, cook over medium heat until the mixture has a thick pudding-like consistency, about 7 minutes.

Remove from heat and stir in vanilla, then fold in tofu and shredded coconut.

Pour filling into pre-baked pie crust, spreading evenly throughout.

Refrigerate until thoroughly chilled and set, at least 8 hours but preferably overnight.

Topping: Heat oven to 325 degrees.

Place coconut and powdered sugar together in a plastic bag. Shake well to coat.

Spread coconut-sugar mixture on an ungreased pan and bake for 3 minutes. Allow to cool.

Spread coconut whipped topping evenly over chilled pie. Then sprinkle with cooled toasted coconut.

Serve drizzled with chocolate sauce (recipe, p. 146).

Store pie in refrigerator.

Desserts

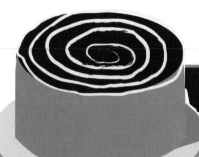

PEANUT BUTTER
PIE

Makes 1 pie

INGREDIENTS

- 1 prebaked store-bought or home-made vegan pie crust (recipe, p. 147)

For Filling
- 1½ cups (1 package) firm silken tofu
- 1 cup roasted & salted creamy peanut butter
- 1 cup vegan sugar
- ½ tsp. vanilla
- ¼ tsp. salt
- ¼ cup cashew cream (recipe, p. 39) or vegan non-dairy cream or non-dairy milk
- 3 Tbs. cornstarch

TO PREPARE

Combine all filling ingredients in a blender or food processor until smooth.

Pour filling into prebaked but cooled pie crust, spreading evenly throughout.

Refrigerate until thoroughly chilled and set, at least 5 hours but preferably overnight.

Serve with tofu whipped topping (recipe, p. 149) and/or drizzle with chocolate sauce (recipe, p. 146).

Store pie in refrigerator.

★ ★ ★

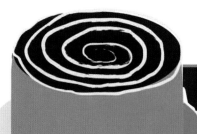

CHOCOLATE CHIP COOKIES

Makes 2 dozen

INGREDIENTS

- ½ cup vegan margarine
- ½ cup vegan sugar
- ½ cup vegan brown sugar
- reconstituted egg replacer powder equal to 1 egg
- 1 tsp. vanilla
- 1¾ cups all-purpose flour
- 1 tsp. baking powder
- ½ tsp. baking soda
- ½ tsp. salt
- 1 cup vegan chocolate chips
- *optional:*
    - 1 cup chopped walnuts

TO PREPARE

Preheat oven to 350 degrees.

Cream together margarine, sugar, brown sugar, egg replacer, and vanilla.

Separately, combine flour, baking powder, baking soda, and salt.

Combine dry and wet ingredients, mixing to make a dough.

Fold in chocolate chips and optional walnuts.

Drop dough by rounded teaspoonful onto a greased baking sheet, about 2 inches apart.

Bake for 8-10 minutes, until cookie bottoms are golden brown.

Desserts

PEANUT BUTTER COOKIES

Makes 2 dozen

INGREDIENTS

- ½ cup vegan margarine
- ½ cup vegan sugar
- ½ cup vegan brown sugar
- ½ cup roasted & salted creamy peanut butter
- reconstituted egg replacer powder equal to 1 egg
- 1 tsp. vanilla
- 1½ cups all-purpose flour
- ½ tsp. baking powder
- ¼ tsp. baking soda
- ½ tsp. salt

TO PREPARE

Preheat oven to 375 degrees.

Cream together margarine, sugar, brown sugar, peanut butter, egg replacer, and vanilla.

Separately, combine flour, baking powder, baking soda, and salt.

Combine dry and wet ingredients, mixing to make a dough.

Shape dough into 1 inch balls and place on ungreased cookie sheet 2 inches apart.

With the tines of a fork, flatten each cookie twice, making a criss-cross pattern.

Bake for 8-10 minutes, or until cookie bottoms are golden brown.

CHOCOLATE LAYER CAKE

Makes 1 cake

INGREDIENTS

For Cake
- 2 cups water
- 3½ cups all-purpose flour
- 2⅔ cups vegan sugar
- 1 cup unsweetened cocoa powder
- 2 tsp. baking powder
- 1½ tsp. baking soda
- 1½ tsp. salt
- 1 tsp. apple cider vinegar
- 1¼ cups canola oil or softened vegan margarine
- reconstituted egg replacer powder equal to 3 eggs
- 1½ tsp. vanilla

For Frosting
- 3¾ cups vegan powdered sugar
- ½ cup unsweetened cocoa powder
- ½ cup vegan margarine
- 1⅓ tsp. vanilla
- 2-4 Tbs. vegan non-dairy cream

TO PREPARE

Preheat oven to 350 degrees.

Grease and flour two 8 inch cake pans.

Cake: Combine flour, sugar, cocoa powder, baking powder, baking soda, and salt.

Separately, combine vinegar, oil or margarine, egg replacer, and vanilla.

Combine dry and wet ingredients, mixing to make a batter (30 seconds on low speed, then 3 minutes on high, scraping sides occasionally).

Pour batter into prepared pans.

Bake for 30 minutes, or until a toothpick inserted into the center comes out clean.

Frosting: While cakes are baking, whip together powdered sugar, cocoa powder, margarine, vanilla, and 2 Tbs. cream with a mixer until smooth and fluffy, stopping several times to scrape the sides of the bowl. If needed, add up to 2 Tbs. more cream to achieve desired consistency.

When cool, flip 1 cake out onto serving platter. Cut off any dry edges and frost top of cake.

Flip second cake onto parchment paper. Cut off any dry edges, then gently place on top of frosted cake. Finish frosting top and sides.

Serve with ice cream (recipes, pp. 142-144).

Desserts

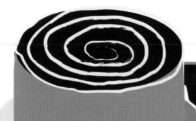

Makes 4 mini-loaf cakes or 18 mini-cupcakes.

INGREDIENTS

For Cake
- 1½ cups non-dairy milk
- 1 Tbs. apple cider vinegar
- 2⅛ cups all-purpose flour
- 2 tsp. baking powder
- ½ tsp. baking soda
- ½ tsp. salt
- ½ cup canola oil
- 1⅛ cups vegan sugar
- 1 tsp. vanilla

For Filling
- ½ cup vegan shortening
- ¼ cup vegan margarine
- 1¼ cup vegan powdered sugar
- 1 tsp. vanilla
- 1 tsp. barley malt syrup
- pinch of salt

Note: Mini-loaf pans or mini-muffin pans are required for this recipe. The loaf pans will create "Twinkies" that are larger than real ones. This recipe also calls for a tool that will allow you to inject the cakes with cream filling. You can use a pastry injector or a cake decorating bag.

TO PREPARE

Preheat oven to 350 degrees.

Cake: Grease and flour mini-loaf or mini-muffin pans.

In a large bowl, combine milk with apple cider vinegar. Set aside for 10 minutes to curdle.

Separately, combine flour, baking powder, baking soda, and salt.

Stir oil, sugar, and vanilla into milk-vinegar mixture.

Combine dry and wet ingredients, mixing to make a batter.

Scoop batter into pans, ¾ full.

Bake loaves for 15-20 minutes and cupcakes for 10-15 minutes, or until a toothpick inserted into the center comes out clean.

Filling: While cakes are baking, whip together all filling ingredients with a mixer on low speed until thoroughly blended, stopping several times to scrape the sides of the bowl. Then whip on highest speed for 2 minutes more, stopping once to scrape the sides of the bowl.

After baking, allow loaves/cupcakes to cool completely, then remove from pans.

Fill pastry injector or cake decorating bag fitted with largest tip with cream filling. Stick tip of pastry injector or cake decorating bag into the bottom of each cooled loaf or cupcake, and gently squeeze.

continued...

If you are filling a mini-loaf, you should aim to place approximately 1½ Tbs. into the loaf three times each (in the center and at each end of the loaf). If you are filling a cupcake, one shot of approximately 2 Tbs. is enough.

VANILLA CUPCAKES

Makes 1 dozen

INGREDIENTS

For Cupcakes
- 2 cups all-purpose flour
- ¼ cup vegan sugar
- 1 tsp. baking powder
- 1 tsp. baking soda
- ½ tsp. salt
- ¼ cup canola oil
- 1 cup maple syrup
- 1 cup non-dairy milk
- 1½ tsp. apple cider vinegar

For Frosting
- 3 cups vegan powdered sugar
- ⅓ cup vegan margarine
- 2 tsp. vanilla
- 1-2 Tbs. vegan non-dairy cream

Optional Topping
  -vegan sprinkles

TO PREPARE

Preheat oven to 350 degrees.

Grease a muffin pan or line with paper baking cups.

Combine flour, sugar, baking powder, baking soda, and salt.

Separately, whisk oil, maple syrup, milk, and vinegar together until foamy.

Combine dry and wet ingredients, mixing to make a batter.

Pour batter into muffin pan or cups.

Bake for 15-20 minutes, or until a toothpick inserted into the center comes out clean.

Frosting: While cupcakes are baking, whip together powdered sugar, margarine, vanilla, and 1 Tbs. cream with a mixer until smooth and fluffy, stopping several times to scrape the sides of the bowl. If needed, add another tablespoon cream to achieve desired consistency.

After cupcakes have thoroughly cooled, spread tops generously with frosting and optional sprinkles.

Desserts

NEW YORK CHEESECAKE

INGREDIENTS

Makes 1 cake

For Crust
- 1 tsp. molasses
- 3½ Tbs. canola oil
- 1 tsp. vanilla
- ¾ cup all-purpose flour
- 1½ Tbs. vegan sugar
- 1 tsp. baking powder
- ¼ tsp. baking soda
- ⅛ tsp. salt

For Filling
- 3 cups (3 8-oz. packages) vegan cream cheese
- 1¾ cups vegan sugar
- 1½ tsp. vanilla
- 2 Tbs. vegan liquid lecithin
- 1½ Tbs. egg replacer powder, dissolved in ½ cup water
- ¾ cup all-purpose flour
- 2 Tbs. lemon zest
- ⅛ tsp. salt
- ¼ cup cashew cream (recipe, p. 39) or vegan non-dairy cream

TO PREPARE

Crust: Preheat oven to 375 degrees.

In a large bowl, combine molasses, oil, and vanilla.

Separately, combine flour, sugar, baking powder, baking soda, and salt.

Combine dry and wet ingredients, mixing to make a course meal.

Spread onto a baking sheet, ½ inch thick.

Bake for 4 minutes. Remove from oven and stir. Return to oven for 3 more minutes.

Break up large lumps, if any, when cooled.

Press crumbled crust mixture, ¼ inch thick, onto the bottom of an 8 or 9 inch pie pan.

Filling: Reduce oven temperature to 300 degrees.

In a large bowl, combine cream cheese and sugar. Then beat at medium speed while slowly adding vanilla, liquid lecithin, dissolved egg replacer, flour, lemon zest, salt, and cream.

Pour into pie pan.

Partially fill a baking dish that is larger than the cheesecake pan with hot water. Place cheesecake within this larger pan. Place both pans, staggered one inside the other, into oven.

Bake 1 hour, or a few minutes more until cake rises a bit and
continued...

the top is golden brown.

Refrigerate until thoroughly chilled and set, at least 10 hours but preferably overnight.

Serve with warmed fruit topping (recipe, p. 122) and/or drizzle with chocolate sauce (recipe, p. 146).

CHOCOLATE PUDDING

Serves 4

INGREDIENTS
- 1½ cups (1 package) firm silken tofu
- ½ cup vegan sugar
- 1 cup vegan semi-sweet chocolate chips, melted
- 1 tsp. vanilla
- 2 Tbs. cornstarch
- ¼ tsp. salt

TO PREPARE
Blend all ingredients in a food processor or blender until smooth and creamy (for tips on melting chocolate, see page 141).

Refrigerate until thoroughly chilled and set, at least 5 hours but preferably overnight.

SERVING SUGGESTIONS
Serve with coconut whipped topping (recipe, p. 148).

FOR A COOKIE PUDDING PARFAIT: In a wine glass, alternate layers of chilled and set pudding and crumbled vegan cookies (recipes, 133-134). Top with coconut whipped topping (recipe, p. 148).

FOR CHOCOLATE CREAM PIE: Double recipe and pour pudding into a pre-baked but cooled pie crust (recipe, p. 147). Refrigerate until thoroughly chilled and set, at least 5 hours but preferably overnight. Top with coconut whipped topping (recipe, p. 148).

FOR CHOCOLATE BANANA CREAM PIE: Line the bottom of a prebaked but cooled pie crust with ¼ inch slices of 2 bananas so they are touching but not overlapping. Pour chocolate pudding on top of banana slices, spreading evenly throughout. Refrigerate until thoroughly chilled and set, at least 5 hours but preferably overnight. Top with coconut whipped topping (recipe, p. 148).

Desserts

PEANUT BUTTER CUPS

Makes 1½ dozen

INGREDIENTS

For Filling
- ¾ cup roasted & salted creamy peanut butter
- 1 cup vegan powdered sugar
- 1 tsp. salt

For Coating
- 10 oz. (1 bag) vegan semi-sweet chocolate chips, melted

Also
- sturdy paper candy cups

It really isn't rocket science. Read the ingredients on a Reese's peanut butter cup package and it couldn't be more straightforward: chocolate, peanut butter, powdered sugar, salt, and of course, some preservatives thrown in for shelf life. So why is it that almost every attempt at a vegan version includes some ingredient that doesn't belong anywhere near a peanut butter cup, corrupting its taste and the sheer joy of eating one? Inexplicably, we've found oatmeal, graham crackers, agave, coconut, whole wheat flour, and of all things, blue-green algae in vegan peanut butter cups. Perhaps they are thrown in to make them seem healthier, and therefore assuage guilt about eating candy. But no one in their right mind eats candy for health.

Thankfully, delicious and totally authentic tasting vegan peanut butter cups are easy to make. As long as you have the fortitude to make it like the original by adding nothing superfluous and not skimping on the salt and sugar, you will be richly rewarded.

TO PREPARE

Combine peanut butter, powdered sugar, and salt, mixing to a clay-like but not sticky consistency. Form the peanut butter mixture into peanut butter disks, aiming for a thickness and diameter just slightly smaller than that of the paper cup (for tips, see next page).

Melt chocolate chips (for tips on melting chocolate, see next page).

Scoop small amounts of chocolate into each paper cup, and spread to evenly cover bottom. Place peanut butter disks into chocolate, and press down lightly. Then cover with another dollop of chocolate, smoothing with a knife to ensure a flat top.

Allow chocolate to harden before serving (placing the cups in the refrigerator will speed this process).

THE PERFECT CHOCOLATE TO PEANUT BUTTER RATIO

Your peanut butter disk should reach as far to the edge, top, and bottom of the cup as possible while allowing for a tiny coating of chocolate surrounding the peanut butter. The disk should fill the majority of the cup, with the top, bottom, and sides of the cup having only a small (at the most ⅛ inch) layer of chocolate. Consider the chocolate to peanut butter ratio in a traditional store-bought peanut butter cup, and try to approximate it as much as possible.

MELTING CHOCOLATE

Most candy recipes call for melting chocolate in a double boiler to ensure that the chocolate does not burn. If you do not have a double boiler, you can always mimic one by placing a small pan inside a larger one partially filled with water. Or you can simply microwave the chocolate. To do so, place the chocolate chips in a bowl and heat for 20-30 seconds. Stir vigorously to transfer the heat until all of the chips have melted.

GEL-OH! PARFAIT

Makes 4

INGREDIENTS

- 1 7-oz. can store-bought vegan whipped topping or 1 batch tofu whipped topping (recipe, p. 149)

For Gel-oh!
- 1 3-oz. box vegan strawberry flavored gel dessert mix
- 1 cup diced strawberries

Optional Toppings
  - vegan candy sprinkles

TO PREPARE

If using tofu whipped topping, prepare it and store in refrigerator until needed.

Gel-oh!: Prepare vegan gel dessert mix according to package directions, stirring in diced strawberries. Refrigerate until thoroughly set.

When set, stir to break up gel so that it is scoopable.

Reblend tofu whipped topping in food processor or with a whisk after removing from refrigerator.

In a wine glass, alternate layers of gel and whipped topping, ending with whipped topping.

Add optional sprinkles.

Desserts

VANILLA ICE CREAM

Makes 1 quart

INGREDIENTS

- 1⅔ cups non-dairy milk
- 1 cup vegan non-dairy cream
- ⅔ cup cashew cream (recipe, p. 39)
- 1 vanilla bean, scored down the middle
- 3 Tbs. cornstarch or arrowroot powder
- ¾ cup vegan sugar
- ½ tsp. salt

Note: Requires an ice cream maker.

TO PREPARE

Pour the milk, cream, and cashew cream into a saucepan and bring to boiling point, then immediately turn off heat.

Add scored vanilla bean and allow it to infuse for 20 minutes.

Separately, whisk together corn starch or arrowroot powder, sugar, and salt.

Remove the vanilla bean from the pan and allow it to cool.

Pour milk-cream mixture into a blender. Scrape the seeds out of the vanilla bean and add to blender. Blend to evenly distribute seeds. Be careful when blending hot liquid, as it can push the lid off of the blender. Place lid on tight, cover with a dish towel, and hold lid down tightly before turning the blender on.

Return milk-cream mixture to the pan and then pour in sugar-corn starch mixture, stirring to combine.

Heat on low until the mixture begins to simmer. Remove from heat and refrigerate until chilled.

Pour into ice cream maker and proceed according to equipment directions.

Serve with coconut or tofu whipped topping (recipes, pp. 148-149), chocolate sauce (recipe, p. 146), or warmed fruit topping (recipe, p. 122). See page 145 for additional serving suggestions.

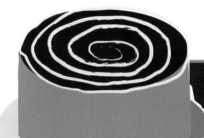

CHOCOLATE ICE CREAM

Makes 1 quart

INGREDIENTS

- 1½ cups (1 package) firm silken tofu
- 1½ cups vegan semi-sweet chocolate chips, melted
- 1 cup vegan non-dairy cream
- 1 tsp. vanilla

Note: Requires an ice cream maker.

TO PREPARE

Blend tofu in a blender or food processor until smooth.

Add the melted chocolate (for tips on melting chocolate, see page 141) and blend thoroughly, scraping sides as needed.

Add cream and vanilla and blend some more.

Pour mixture into a covered container and refrigerate until chilled.

Pour into ice cream maker and proceed according to equipment directions.

Serve with coconut or tofu whipped topping (recipes, pp. 148-149), chocolate sauce (recipe, p. 146), or warmed fruit topping (recipe, p. 122). See page 145 for additional serving suggestions.

Desserts

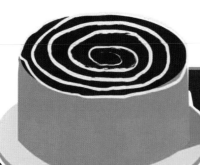

STRAWBERRY ICE CREAM

Makes 1 quart

INGREDIENTS

- 1½ cups diced fresh or frozen strawberries
- 1½ cups vegan non-dairy cream
- ½ cup non-dairy milk
- ⅔ cup vegan sugar
- 1 Tbs. vanilla
- 3 Tbs. cornstarch or arrowroot powder
- ¼ tsp. salt

Note: Requires an ice cream maker.

TO PREPARE

Combine all ingredients in a blender until smooth.

Chill if needed.

Pour into ice cream maker and proceed according to equipment directions.

Serve with coconut or tofu whipped topping (recipes, pp. 148-149), chocolate sauce (recipe, p. 146), or warmed fruit topping (recipe, p. 122). See page 145 for additional serving suggestions.

Desserts

ICE CREAM SERVING SUGGESTIONS

MILKSHAKE

Combine vegan ice cream and non-dairy milk in a blender at a 4 scoop to 1 cup ratio. Drizzle sides of serving glass with chocolate sauce before pouring. Top with whipped topping.

ROOT BEER FLOAT

Place a large scoop of vanilla ice cream in a mug and pour in vegan root beer. Add a straw and a long skinny spoon.

ICE CREAM SUNDAE

Top several scoops of ice cream with whipped topping, chocolate sauce, crushed peanuts, sprinkles, and a cherry.

APPLE PIE À LA MODE

Top a slice of warm apple pie with a scoop of vanilla ice cream.

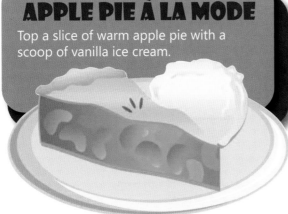

Desserts

CHOCOLATE SAUCE

Makes ¾ cup

INGREDIENTS

- 4 oz. unsweetened chocolate
- 3 Tbs. vegan margarine
- ½ cup water
- ⅔ cup vegan sugar
- 6 Tbs. corn syrup
- pinch of salt
- 1 Tbs. vanilla
- *optional flavorings*
  - 1 Tbs. vegan rum*
  - 1 Tbs. vegan brandy*
  - 1 Tbs. espresso
  - ½ tsp. mint extract plus 2 crushed vegan candy canes

Beer, wine, and other alcoholic beverages are often made using animal-derived ingredients. Go to allamericanvegan.com for a list of vegan-friendly beers, wines, and spirits.

TO PREPARE

Heat chocolate and margarine in a double boiler or in the microwave, stirring frequently until melted (for tips on melting chocolate, see page 141).

Separately, heat water to boiling in a small saucepan.

Stir chocolate-margarine mixture into water, then add sugar, corn syrup, and salt.

Stirring constantly, cook until mixture starts to boil. Adjust heat so that sauce is maintained at this boiling point, and cook for 9 minutes.

Allow to cool for 15 minutes. Stir in vanilla and other optional flavorings.

Serve warm over ice cream (recipes, pp. 142-144) or drizzle over pie (recipes, pp. 130-132).

Note: To reheat sauce, microwave for 15-30 seconds. Stir well and it will regain shine and proper consistency.

PIE CRUST

*Makes 1 or 2
8 inch pie crusts*

INGREDIENTS

For 1 pie crust
- 1¼ cups all-purpose flour
- ½ tsp. salt
- ½ tsp. vegan sugar
- ½ cup vegan margarine or vegan shortening, chilled
- 2-3 Tbs. ice water

For 2 pie crusts
- 2½ cups all-purpose flour
- 1 tsp. salt
- 1 tsp. vegan sugar
- 1 cup vegan margarine or vegan shortening, chilled
- 4-6 Tbs. ice water

TO PREPARE

In a food processor, combine flour, salt, and sugar and pulse to mix.

Add margarine or shortening, divided into several spoonfuls, and pulse 6-8 times until mixture resembles coarse meal.

Add ice water 1 Tbs. at a time, pulsing until mixture begins to clump together. If dough sticks together and holds its shape when you pinch it, it's done. If not, add more water and pulse again.

Remove dough and place in a mound on a lightly floured surface and form into a ball. If making 2 crusts, divide dough and gently shape into 2 equal sized balls. Wrap (each) ball in plastic wrap and refrigerate for 1 hour.

Remove dough from refrigerator and allow to sit at room temperature for 10 minutes to soften.

Roll dough out on a lightly floured surface, making ⅛ inch thick circle that is slightly larger than pie pan.

Carefully transfer to a pie pan and gently press into place. Fold edges back over and flute.

To prebake: If recipe calls for a prebaked crust, bake at 375 degrees until it begins to color around the edges, about 15 minutes. To ensure that the pie crust does not rise while baking, prick sides and bottom of crust in several places to allow steam to escape, or place a sheet of parchment paper, covered with dried beans or pie weights, inside the pie crust before baking.

Desserts

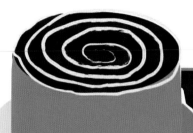

COCONUT WHIPPED TOPPING

Makes 1¾ cups

INGREDIENTS

- 13 oz. (1 can) coconut milk (regular, not light, with no emulsifiers)
- 1 cup vegan powdered sugar

TO PREPARE

Refrigerate can of coconut milk for at least 8 hours.

Place a large metal bowl and blender beaters in refrigerator to chill for at least 30 minutes.

Take coconut milk out of refrigerator and make a small opening in the bottom of the can with can opener. Let liquid drain out entirely (you will not use this liquid).

Once the can is drained, open can and scoop out coconut fat, removing to chilled mixing bowl.

With chilled blender beaters, whip in powdered sugar. Do not overmix.

If you are using this topping in one of the pie recipes, be sure the pie is cooled before applying or it will melt. To apply as the top layer of a pie, place topping in cake decorating bag set with largest tip and spread evenly over pie, or dollop several large spoonfuls of topping on pie with a spoon, then gently spread out with knife or spatula to create an even layer.

Store in refrigerator until ready to serve.

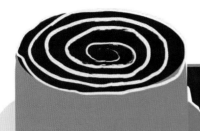

TOFU WHIPPED TOPPING

Makes 2 cups

INGREDIENTS

- ⅓ cup apple juice
- 1 Tbs. agar flakes*
- pinch of salt plus ¼ tsp. more, divided
- 1½ cups (1 package) firm silken tofu
- 1 tsp. vanilla
- ½ cup vegan sugar

Agar is a tasteless vegan gelatin substitute made from seaweed. Look for it in the Japanese section of your natural food store.

TO PREPARE

Combine apple juice, agar, and a pinch of salt in a small saucepan over medium heat. Bring to a boil, reduce heat to low, cover and cook until the agar dissolves, about 4 minutes, stirring occasionally.

Separately, combine tofu, vanilla, sugar, and ¼ tsp. salt in a food processor until smooth.

When agar is dissolved, add apple juice-agar mixture to food processor and blend.

Cover and refrigerate until set, about one hour. Reblend in food processor immediately before use.

Serve in gel-oh! parfait (recipe, p. 141) or over ice cream (recipes, pp. 142-144).

All American Vegan Thanksgiving

STUFFED NOT A TURKEY WITH
MAPLE GLAZED ROOT VEGETABLES 152

MASHED POTATOES 109
WITH GRAVY 124

CRESCENT ROLLS 155

CANDIED YAMS 156

CRANBERRY SAUCE 157

WALDORF SALAD 158

PUMPKIN PIE 159

Thank You!

**A Thanksgiving dinner turkeys
can be grateful for, too.**

Thanksgiving

STUFFED NOT A TURKEY WITH MAPLE GLAZED ROOT VEGETABLES

INGREDIENTS

Serves 8

Note: This recipe requires approximately 5 hours to prepare.

For Stuffing
- 9 slices vegan bread
- ½ medium yellow onion, chopped
- 2 celery stalks, diced
- 4 Tbs. vegan margarine
- ⅛ cup minced fresh parsley
- ½ tsp. dried ground sage
- ½ tsp. dried thyme
- ¼ tsp. salt
- ½ tsp. black pepper
- 1 cup vegan chicken broth
- ½ tsp. egg replacer powder
- 2 Tbs. water
- *optional:*
   - ⅓ cup raisins

For Root Vegetables
- 2 large russet potatoes, chopped
- 1 large yam, chopped
- 3 large carrots, chopped
- 1 medium beet, chopped
- 4 Tbs. olive oil
- 1 tsp. salt
- ½ tsp. black pepper

For Glaze
- 1 cup vegetable broth
- 1 Tbs. balsamic vinegar
- 2 Tbs. maple syrup
- 2 Tbs. vegan margarine

For Not a Turkey
- vegan chicken flavored concentrated stock or bouillon (see preparation instructions for amount)
- 2 cups hot water
- 4 Tbs. cashew cream (recipe, p. 39)
- 2½ cups wheat gluten flour
- ¼ cup soy flour
- ⅛ cup oat flour
- ¼ cup nutritional yeast
- 1 very large russet potato

For Simmering Broth
- 8 cups hot vegan chicken broth (either premade or reconstituted according to package directions)
- 1 cup cashew cream
- 1 cup sliced mushrooms
- 1 tsp. minced garlic
- ½ tsp. onion powder
- ⅛ tsp. celery seed
- 1 bay leaf
- 1 Tbs. olive oil

TO PREPARE

STEP 1
STUFFING

Note: This recipe makes enough stuffing to fill the not a turkey only. If you want more stuffing to serve separately, double the recipe.

Preheat oven to 400 degrees.

Lay bread slices flat on baking sheet. Do not overlap.

Bake bread until golden brown, 6-8 minutes.

When cool, cut bread into ½ inch cubes.

Reduce oven temperature to 350 degrees.

In a large skillet, sauté onions and celery in margarine until tender.

In a large bowl, mix together bread, onion-celery mixture, and remaining stuffing ingredients.

Pour into a greased loaf pan.

Cover with foil and bake for 30 minutes.

Refrigerate until needed.

STEP 2
VEGETABLES

Preheat oven to 400 degrees.

Toss chopped vegetables in a bowl with olive oil, salt, and black pepper.

Pour into a large, shallow baking dish, then bake for 30 minutes until tender and light brown. Meanwhile, begin glaze.

Glaze: In a small saucepan, combine broth, vinegar, and maple syrup and bring to a boil. Cook until reduced to ¼ cup, about 12 minutes. Remove from heat and whisk in margarine.

When vegetables are done baking, scoop them into a large bowl. Pour glaze over vegetables and stir to coat.

Adjust salt to taste.

Refrigerate until needed.

STEP 3
NOT A TURKEY

Preheat oven to 300 degrees.

Grease a large mixing bowl with olive oil and wipe off excess.

In greased bowl, dissolve vegan chicken stock or bouillon in hot water, doubling the amount recommended by product label per cup. For example, if stock or bouillon requires 1 tsp. per 1 cup water to reconstitute, add 2 tsp. per cup instead. Since the recipe calls for 2 cups of water, you would therefore add 4 tsp. total.

continued...

STEP 3
NOT A TURKEY, CONTINUED

Do not use a premade liquid stock for this step, as it will not have enough flavor concentration.

Add cashew cream and stir to combine.

Separately, combine wheat gluten flour, soy flour, oat flour, and nutritional yeast.

Combine dry and wet ingredients, mixing for 2 minutes until the gluten is activated and the ingredients stick together to form a dough. If mixing by hand, grease hands with olive oil to prevent sticking.

Simmering Broth: In a large stockpot, bring all simmering broth ingredients to a boil and turn off heat. Pour simmering broth into a Dutch oven (unless stockpot is oven-safe).

Grease hands with olive oil and shape seitan into a large, flat circle. Wrap potato in seitan at a uniform thickness. Pinch edges together to fully seal.

Place seitan ball into simmering broth, seam side down, adding heated broth as necessary to ensure that seitan is fully submerged. For every additional ½ cup of broth added, include 1 extra Tbs. of cashew cream.

Cover and bake for 2 hours. During the last 20 minutes of baking, place covered stuffing and covered maple glazed vegetables into oven to warm.

Remove seitan, stuffing, and vegetables from oven.

Remove seitan from broth to a large plate or cutting board. Flip to bottom, and make the smallest cut possible to remove potato. Fill cavity with stuffing.

Place not a turkey right side up on a large serving platter. Distribute vegetables evenly around the outside of the not a turkey as a colorful garnish.

Serve with gravy (recipe, p. 124).

Thanksgiving

CRESCENT ROLLS

Makes 2 dozen

INGREDIENTS

- 4 tsp. (2 packets) active dry yeast
- 1 Tbs. plus ½ cup vegan sugar, divided
- 1 cup warm water
- 3 tsp. egg replacer powder
- ½ cup melted but cooled* vegan margarine plus more for brushing
- 4 cups all-purpose flour, divided
- 1 tsp. salt

Cool or yeast could deactivate.

TO PREPARE

Dissolve yeast in warm water with 1 Tbs. sugar and let stand for 5-10 minutes to proof (yeast should foam).

Combine dissolved yeast with ½ cup sugar, egg replacer powder, cooled melted margarine, 2 cups flour, and salt and beat together. Mix in remaining 2 cups flour and more as needed to create a dough that is smooth and not sticky.

Place in a well-greased bowl, flip, cover with a damp kitchen towel or plastic wrap and let rise until doubled in size, about 1½ hours.

Divide dough in half and roll each half out (one at a time) into a circle with a diameter of 12 inches. Brush with margarine and then cut dough like a pizza into 12 wedges.

Starting at the large rounded edge, roll each slice of dough up to the tip. Lay each roll on a greased or parchment paper-lined baking tray with small tip facing down and tucked underneath the roll, and the ends curved in toward the center, forming a crescent shape. Cover with a tea towel or cloth napkin and let rise for 1 hour.

Preheat oven to 400 degrees.

Bake 8 minutes; brush with margarine, and return to oven for 3-4 minutes more or until golden brown.

Serve warm.

Thanksgiving

CANDIED YAMS

Serves 6

INGREDIENTS

- 3 large yams
- ⅓ cup vegan margarine plus 1 Tbs. more, divided into several dollops
- ½ tsp. salt
- ½ tsp. black pepper
- ⅓ cup maple syrup
- ¼ cup orange juice
- 2 cups bite-sized or quartered large vegan marshmallows

TO PREPARE

Preheat oven to 400 degrees.

Bake yams until tender. Begin testing after 45 minutes.

When cool enough to handle, peel and slice yams into chunks then thoroughly mash.

Combine yams, ⅓ cup margarine, salt, black pepper, maple syrup, and orange juice, mixing until smooth.

Spread evenly in a greased shallow baking dish.

Dot with dollops of margarine, then top with marshmallows.

Bake for 25-30 minutes, or until all of the marshmallows are puffy and golden brown.

Thanksgiving

CRANBERRY SAUCE

Serves 8

INGREDIENTS

- 1 cup water
- 1 cup vegan sugar
- 2 cups cranberries
- 1 Tbs. finely grated orange zest

TO PREPARE

Combine water and sugar in a saucepan.

Heat to boiling then cook for 5 minutes.

Stir in cranberries.

Bring to a boil again and cook for another 5 minutes, stirring occasionally.

Remove from heat, stir in orange zest and refrigerate for at least 8 hours before serving.

Thanksgiving

WALDORF SALAD

Serves 6

INGREDIENTS

- ⅔ cup vegan mayonnaise
- 2 tsp. lemon juice
- ½ tsp. salt
- ½ tsp. black pepper
- 2 apples, cored and diced into ½ inch chunks
- 1 cup diced celery
- 1 cup quartered red seedless grapes
- 1 cup toasted then chopped walnuts

TO PREPARE

Preheat oven to 350 degrees.

Spread walnuts on an ungreased pan and bake for 5 minutes. Allow to cool, then chop into ¼ inch pieces and measure to 1 cup.

Separately, combine mayonnaise, lemon juice, salt, and black pepper.

Mix in apples, celery, grapes, and toasted and chopped walnuts.

Thanksgiving

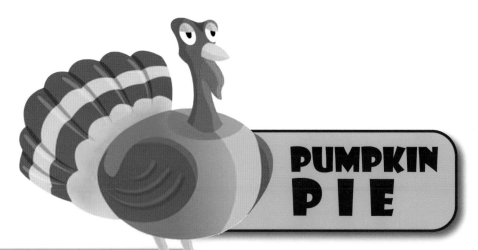

PUMPKIN PIE

Makes 1 pie

INGREDIENTS

- 1 unbaked store-bought or home-made pie crust (recipe, p. 147)

For Filling
- 1½ cups (1 package) firm silken tofu
- 15 oz. pureed pumpkin
- ⅓ cup canola oil
- ½ tsp. molasses
- ⅔ cup vegan sugar
- 1½ tsp. cinnamon
- ¾ tsp. ginger powder
- ½ tsp. nutmeg
- ⅛ tsp. ground cloves
- ½ tsp. salt
- ½ tsp. vanilla

TO PREPARE

Preheat oven to 350 degrees.

Blend tofu in a blender or food processor until smooth.

Add remaining filling ingredients to blender, mixing until smooth.

Pour filling into pie crust.

Bake for 55 minutes.

Refrigerate until thoroughly chilled and set, at least 8 hours but preferably overnight.

Serve with tofu whipped topping (recipe, p. 149).

Let Them Eat Cake

As an animal rights activist living in the twenty-first century, it is easy to feel like a stranger in a strange land. With a lifestyle at odds with that of most people and a belief that an infinitely more compassionate society is possible, we confess there are times we wish we'd been born at a later date, in the brighter future our great-grandchildren, or perhaps their children, will inherit. In that future, everyone will be vegan, animals will enjoy the same rights and protections we afford our fellow humans, and the world we live in today will be viewed as a cruel aberration of the past. We are certain that day will come eventually, but the longer it takes, the greater the suffering and the higher the body count. Our job as animal activists is therefore to hasten its arrival. But how?

Many of Albert Einstein's theories began as thought experiments, a simple imagining of "what if?" What would happen to the Earth's orbit if the Sun suddenly disappeared? What would the world look like if he chased a beam of light? Einstein credited these efforts with his greatest discoveries, including his Theory of Relativity. Could thought experiments help those who work on social justice issues, such as animal rights? We think so. Our collective journey toward animal liberation begins with imagining the world we want to create, believing it is possible to achieve, and then fostering the necessary changes to make that dream a reality. It is a forward-looking journey that begins, perhaps ironically, with a motivating backward glance.

To paraphrase abolitionist Theodore Parker and Dr. Martin Luther King, Jr., the arc of history is long, but it bends toward greater justice. The past reveals that although violence, intolerance, and prejudice have been endemic to our history, we have demonstrated the capacity to overcome our darker natures. So while it is easy to get discouraged by the sheer number of animals killed in a bewildering array of contexts, one need only study the astounding achievements of other social justice movements to feel exhilarated by our prospects for success. We must start with the conviction that we can achieve a more humane, compassionate society—a *vegan* society—and then set our sights on building the infrastructure to move our culture from where it is now to where we want it to be. We must build a bridge that connects our world with this brighter future.

To do so we must start by determining how such a future would differ from ours, so that we can understand the changes we need to bring about. One way we can do this is to imagine what a person from that future, coming back to our own era, would think about *our* society. What things we accept as inevitable because of prevalence, custom, and familiarity would they know to be otherwise? What things about our culture would seem shocking, perplexing, even cruel to a person coming from an era in which such myopia and limitations have already been overcome and more humane ways prevail?

Transported from a world in which humans no longer eat animals or their products, and animals enjoy the rights and protections which activists today struggle to achieve on their behalf, our time traveler would be free of the prejudices and rationalizations that reconcile us to the atrocities we routinely inflict on non-human animals with ruthless efficiency. A person from this future would express sadness and anger at our treatment of animals, much like we would feel were we to go back and witness slavery in the antebellum South. But what is more significant for the purposes of this discussion is what they would think about the way most people cook, the things most restaurants serve, and the products which line most supermarket shelves. Coming from an era in which people no longer consume animals and their products, what would our traveler know about the possibilities of veganism that may be hard for us, trapped in our own time, to recognize or conceptualize?

Admittedly, it can seem like pure conjecture to play this game—to imagine what would be eaten in a totally vegan society. But following Einstein's approach, we can make educated guesses, based on knowledge we already have. That is, we can infer what is most likely to succeed, given our knowledge of the foods most people today already enjoy eating, those foods which help today's vegans remain dedicated vegans, and which even non-vegans often enjoy.

Most vegan foods being produced and sold today are analogs, imitating staples of the American diet: products like veggie burgers, veggie dogs, non-dairy ice creams, soymilks, and vegan cheeses. As these analogs improve and become indistinguishable in taste and tex-

> One can imagine the shock our time traveler would feel by our reliance on animals as "food," or ingredients in "food," in ways completely unnecessary to achieve the end result for which they are used.

ture from the original, they will eventually become more widespread. In a vegan society, we can assume that the success of veganism is due, in large part, to this perfection having been achieved, and to the wider availability of these foods. And given that these foods reflect how most Americans eat today, it doesn't take a rocket scientist—or a time traveler—to connect the dots. It simply makes sense, and is pretty safe to assume, that our future traveler would be dumbfounded at our failure to recognize and collectively act upon what to her seems so obvious: that all the foods we now eat can be made in a way in which no one is killed and the planet isn't polluted.

One can imagine the shock our time traveler would feel wandering through the food court in a contemporary American mall, astounded by our reliance on animals as "food," or ingredients in "food," in ways completely unnecessary to achieve the end result for which they are used. *What are they thinking?* she might wonder. *Why all the flesh of animals when meat analogs are possible? Why all the eggs and dairy products as mere ingredients, when the purpose they serve in a particular recipe is so easily replaced?*

Between now and then, big changes will have occurred. These will likely include responses to climate change, a humanitarian food crisis, and the passage of laws reflecting greater concern for the welfare and rights of animals. But we believe that the biggest factor, and the one now most neglected by the animal rights movement, is the seemingly more mundane expansion and greater availability of delicious alternatives to meat, eggs, and dairy products.

Most of the innovation occurring in vegan foods is happening within natural food companies, only a few of which produce solely vegan foods. Most, however, produce just a few vegan foods, and sometimes do so inadvertently. Vegan foods are now produced primarily either by chance or by companies seeking to appeal to the relatively small portion of the American market that wants to eat "health" foods.

Currently, there is not one, large, powerful force deliberately steering a course towards the more widespread production and distribution of appealing ready-made vegan foods. It is a void that desperately needs filling and the answer as to who should do so seems obvious when you consider who stands the most to gain by its achievement: the animal rights movement.

Right now the animal rights community is promoting the idea that people should not eat animals without ensuring that there are widely available alternatives for people to eat instead.

Right now the animal rights community is promoting the idea that people should not eat animals without ensuring that there are widely available alternatives for people to eat *instead*. These products are not promoted aggressively, and when they are it is usually only to other vegans. The animal rights movement also plays virtually no role in their production and distribution. To create a compassionate society, we don't need "free range" chickens; we need "chickenless" chickens. We do not envision a future in which widespread veganism means that everyone eats nothing but fruits and vegetables. We instead imagine a future in which everyone eats the same foods we eat now but delicious vegan versions of them, and people don't miss the old days but rather shudder in horror at the thought of them.

Render Animal Products Obsolete

The environmental movement has had its share of successes and failures. One area where it has been unsuccessful is in getting people to give up their gas-powered, oversized cars. The reason its success has been limited is that, while there will always be people who buy smaller, more fuel-efficient hybrid or electric cars, who take mass transit even when it is haphazard and time-consuming, and who ride bicycles instead of drive cars, this contingent is decidedly in the minority. They are what vegans are today—those who are willing to do what is right regardless of whether it is easy or not to do so. In other words, they are willing to embrace a lifestyle that is inconvenient compared to the status quo. Statistics show that the vast majority of Americans, regardless of political affiliation, claim to be concerned about the environment, but they still drive fossil-fuel-dependent cars. To get Americans out of

their gas-guzzling SUVs, we can't offer them funky-looking, tiny electric vehicles. We need to offer them electric cars that look the same, cost the same, run the same, and are available at the same places.

Likewise, a majority of Americans care about animals, but still eat meat. The animal rights movement needs to comprehensively expand vegan options and the awareness of how to use them so that, ultimately, animal-based products are rendered obsolete because their cost will be recognized as too high a price to pay when ethical alternatives are abundantly available and identical in taste.

Imagine entire departments of the largest animal protection organizations, which already have tens of millions and even hundreds of millions of dollars in annual revenues, dedicated to transforming the American landscape to make it more vegan-friendly. To do that, they could have in-house Research and Development teams staffed by chemists and chefs producing cutting-edge vegan analogs. Once such products are developed, they could sell the foods themselves or share their discoveries with food companies that have national distribution. They could have staff members dedicated to meeting with and educating food companies about how to replace non-vegan ingredients in their products with alternatives so that we can begin to veganize America's favorite brand-name foods.

> Imagine entire departments of the largest animal protection organizations dedicated to transforming the American landscape to make it more vegan-friendly.

Animal rights groups could focus on increasing the variety of vegan foods in public venues. They could invest in chains of fast food vegan restaurants. They could create culinary institutes that provide chefs with continuing education in vegan cooking and the art of vegan substitution. They could encourage vegan options on every restaurant menu by having representatives meet with chefs across the country, offering them delicious vegan recipes for every course (no steamed vegetables over rice, please!). And they could promote vegan-friendly restaurants and have campaigns to create vegan-friendly cities.

Imagine an incentive-based campaign such as "Vegan Nashville" or "Vegan Omaha" that set out to expand vegan options in a particular city. Such a campaign could have certain benchmarks a city must meet in order to earn the distinction of being "vegan-friendly" and be promoted accordingly. These benchmarks could include clearly labeled vegan options on restaurant menus, vegan options at school cafeterias, vegan-friendly tourist accommodations, and more.

In an era of mass consumerism, national animal rights organizations could promote vegan products to give them wider appeal.* Vegan "wiener mobiles" and ice cream trucks could travel across the country offering free samples of veggie dogs, veggie burgers, vegan ice cream, and other vegan treats. Cash-strapped schools could be given subsidized vegan lunches to create new generations of future vegans. Animal rights groups

---

*Some animal rights groups do some of these things. Generally speaking, however, when these groups promote vegan products, they are mostly talking to other vegans or aspiring vegans. We need to start talking to non-vegans.

could offer free vegan cooking classes around the country, introducing people to the concept of vegan substitution. They could push for vegan labeling laws that, like kosher certifications, would make identifying vegan products quick and easy. Billboards could draw attention to how easy it is to replace meat, eggs, and dairy products with vegan alternatives, as well as how familiar and delicious vegan food can be. And animal rights groups could create and expand opportunities for people to meet and fall in love with rescued pigs, chickens, and cows.

All this is just the tip of the iceberg. The animal rights movement could be doing so much more beyond the current focus on philosophically converting people to veganism, and, as with California's Proposition 2, seeking legislation that *limits* the harm caused by an animal-based diet. These latter efforts are an important part of our movement's advocacy but they are not enough because they do not seek to eliminate the greatest roadblock preventing more people from eating vegan: the infrastructure we have inherited that favors the eating of animals and their products, and that therefore makes it hard, rather than easy, for people to do the right thing.

You Say You Want a Revolution

When we first became vegan, we liked to imagine a vegan revolution toppling the status quo and ushering in a new era of compassion for animals in one fell swoop. Looking to other social justice movements for guidance, however, we've come to realize that it is highly unlikely that widespread veganism will occur at some seminal, singular moment in time. Instead, it will be the result of cumulative changes in society that make its prospects more probable, and it will be fostered primarily, we believe, by product innovation of meat, eggs, and dairy analogs that will increasingly render animal-based "foods" obsolete.

We've also come to appreciate that social movements often make progress in generational leaps. As young people come of age at a time when particular mores are being publicly reevaluated, they often internalize and then reflect newer, more progressive values. Before Dr. King, an entire generation of Americans was openly racist. The Civil Rights movement forced people to reexamine those views, and it forced our country to enact social policies to combat prejudice. The generation that followed grew up believing that skin color should not prevent equal opportunity, but they too had their blind spots. It was not until gay rights activists like Harvey Milk forced the issue and well-known figures such as Ellen DeGeneres came out in a very public way that homophobia was also revealed to be bigotry. And it became obvious that this new generation's view was far from egalitarian. Today's young people are growing up with openly gay friends and many gay role models in popular culture. They are rejecting the intolerance of their parents, who earlier had rejected the intolerance of theirs.

The sooner a progressive idea is publicly debated, the sooner a generation of Americans is forced to grow up thinking about it. Right now most Americans do not reflect on the ethics of eating animals. For them it is just the way the world is, no different than the once popular but now antiquated idea that white people are superior. The more successful the animal rights movement becomes at forcing an awareness of veganism, the sooner we can create generation gaps necessary for veganism and animal rights to flourish.

Having been constantly exposed to vegan products and vegan advocacy growing up, young people, when they become adults, will not have the same fear or suspicion of change on this issue that too often characterizes older generations when the status quo is challenged. Instead, they will grow up understanding that veganism is a viable alternative to a diet based on animal suffering. They will realize that eating animals is a *choice*. And the sooner that happens, the sooner a subsequent generation will realize, given the cruelty and suffering inherent in an animal-based diet, that it is no choice at all.

> People will realize that eating animals is a *choice*. And the sooner that happens, the sooner a subsequent generation will realize, given the cruelty and suffering inherent in an animal-based diet, that it is no choice at all.

Combined with parallel efforts to stop a national health crisis brought about by our diets and a global environmental crisis fueled by animal agriculture, veganism will eventually reach a critical mass, and not eating animals will become the new norm. When that happens, the concern most people have for animals will take precedence in our public discourse, and the time will be ripe for vegan laws and policies. And we will no longer live in a world in which people can rationalize the ideas that they care about the plight of pigs and also eat them. We will have successfully arrived at the brighter future of our thought experiment, on the road we paved that led there.

Better Living Through Chemistry

Some vegans have at least one or two non-vegan foods for which they still pine. For us it was the Snickers bar. For nearly twenty years we waited patiently, and one day just a few years ago it happened. A new vegan candy bar company came into existence and began churning out versions of Milky Way, Almond Joy, Three Musketeers, and—oh joy—Snickers! Desperate to learn all we could about these new creations, where to buy them, and what people who sampled them were saying—*please be delicious, please be delicious, please be delicious**—we Googled them and ended up on the website of a vegan blogger with a contest offering free samples as a prize.

After years of contenting ourselves with plain dark chocolate, we hoped the vegan community would unanimously rejoice at these candy bars, chock full as they are of the caramel and nougat we all sacrificed when we went vegan. But there they were, raining on everyone's parade, just as we had feared they would be—the vegan health police admonishing the blogger for promoting "junk food."

From the standpoint of what cows must endure on dairy farms, here was what could only be described as tremendously good news—non-dairy alternatives to America's most popular candy bars *but without the cruelty*. Yet the feedback section of the blog was filled with comments by vegans who were downright hostile or preaching caution about whether we should support such products because they are candy. *Spit take!*

Vegans come from all walks of life, and there are many reasons why people choose to become vegan. Some do it out of concern for animals, some for the environment, some for health reasons, and others for all of these reasons combined. Whatever the motivation, every vegan is one less person creating a demand for products that harm animals, and for that those of us who are vegan for ethical reasons should be grateful to our health or environmentally-driven vegan comrades. In many ways our different motivations complement one another, each of us bringing to light all the compelling reasons to embrace veganism. But not always.

There are times when our different motivations can put us at cross-purposes. Those who advocate veganism for ethical reasons cannot afford to be dogmatic about prevailing views regarding what constitutes "health" food. We are duty-bound to support effective means that offer an end to the brutal treatment and killing of

---

*They are!

animals such as vegan replacements for foods that Americans traditionally eat.

When new alternatives are introduced into the market that do not meet the requirements of vegans whose focus is health, perhaps because the fat, sugar, or sodium content of the product or recipe is too high to qualify as "health food," it is wrong for health-oriented vegans to label their promotion by ethically-motivated vegans as hypocritical. It is nothing of the sort. While our means of achieving our ends may be identical—veganism—our goals, in reality, are very different: one seeks to promote healthier eating; the other, an end to the deliberate killing of animals.

Of course, the irony behind this discussion is that the promotion of vegan convenience foods, being the most expedient means of getting people off animal products, is also the most effective means of weaning Americans from those foods that cause them the greatest harm. The debate is thus illusory, with both animals *and* people standing to gain by ready-made vegan foods. All vegans consequently should be on guard against dogmas that ignore the larger good.

Right now, due to technological advances within the flavoring industry, the ability exists to create flavors that taste identical to the animal-based product they are simulating. Every flavor we taste is the result of a particular arrangement of molecules that the brain, through our taste buds and olfactory nerves, identifies and recognizes. The combination of molecules, for example, that our brain identifies as "strawberry" are different from those our brain recognizes as "vanilla."

Were you to visit a laboratory where many of the flavorings that end up in our food and drinks are made, you would see rows of bottles containing various molecular compounds. Those molecules selected to create a strawberry flavor can be the same type of molecules found in a real strawberry, even though the former was manufactured in a laboratory and the latter in a strawberry patch. Our bodies are not able to distinguish where these molecules are coming from, and we metabolize them in the same way.

The flavorings being used in many of the meat analogs available today are primarily derived from yeasts, but they are often the same molecular compounds found in the animal-based product they are replacing. For the most part the products using these flavorings are manufactured by natural food companies that abide by certain criteria to appeal to their perceived niche market sector, people who want to eat healthier foods. Therefore, when they hire flavoring companies, they are very specific as to the criteria that must be met, including limited processing, limited ingredients, and nothing artificial.

These conditions, however, can limit a product's ability to be as authentic tasting as possible. In order to make meat and dairy analogs identical to the animal-based product they are replacing in terms of flavor, texture, and color, more ingredients and processing are often required. After all, to transform a soybean into an authentic looking and authentic tasting piece of meat, you need to do things to it. This "doing things" is called "processing." Unfortunately, for many vegans "processing" and "flavorings" have become dirty words.

Today's prepackaged vegan foods taste good. But they are not always identical to the animal-based product they are replacing. Americans are used to the taste and texture of foods high in fat, sodium, and sugar and they are willing to eat a chicken nugget made up of chemicals and left over body parts. If we insist that they only eat traditional "health" foods in addition to no longer eating animals, we create two obstacles we must overcome to help animals instead of just one. If the ability exists to create identical tasting vegan alternatives to the animal-based foods most Americans currently eat, even if it requires additional flavors and additional processing, we owe it to animals to see that these products are produced and marketed.

Unfortunately, with profit being the bottom line for natural food companies, and given their belief that most of their clientele are driven by health as opposed to ethical imperatives, these companies won't risk alienating customers by engaging in the processing required to make their products as authentic as possible and therefore also appealing to the average American palate. Such innovation is less likely to happen sooner rather than later unless there is a demand for it, a demand that some vegans are not helping to bring about by

We stand at an intersection of two exciting developments in history. The will to stop eating animals is increasing, and the technology that allows us to make that transition in a logical, comfortable, and therefore more achievable way is now at our disposal.

publicly denigrating such products or failing to grasp their significance. As long as these biases persist, the potential for authentic taste in vegan convenience foods will not be achieved, and tools vital to getting Americans to stop eating animals will remain out of reach.

So while we work to increase product lines and product availability, we must also push for true authenticity in taste, texture, and color, even if it means processing, so long as all ingredients are vegan. Not only will such foods have lower pesticide residues and be free of cholesterol, hormones, and antibiotics, but people who are used to eating at the top of the "food chain" will be eating analogs made from the bottom. That is good for animals, good for people, and good for the planet.

We live in an era in which veganism can be *all* things to *all* people. It can accommodate those who love ready-made, convenient, and even "junk" food while making them better off than they would otherwise be by providing identical-tasting vegan alternatives. It also can accommodate the health food crowd by using organic, locally grown, seasonally available, and minimally processed ingredients. Too often our activism promotes a version of veganism that appeals primarily to people in the latter group, when the vast majority of people in this country fall into the former.

Someday that dichotomy may vanish, and if so, we believe that ready-made vegan foods will be one of the important reasons why the American diet moves in a more healthful as well as ethical direction. When that day comes, vegan foods made to accommodate the American palate of today can easily be made to accommodate whatever cultural shifts influence our collective eating habits in the future. If the vegan foods we use to provide a bridge to that future do not meet optimal standards of what constitutes "health" food, so be it. Pragmatism bent on success should be our guide, rather than ineffectual and unyielding dogma that is out of touch with everyday American eating habits.*

We stand at an intersection of two exciting developments. The will to stop eating animals is increasing, and the technology that allows us to make that transition in a logical, comfortable, and therefore more achievable way is now at our disposal. We must seize the opportunity afforded by these developments and give our fellow Americans a taste of what they won't be missing.

Toward a Humane Environmentalism

With the widespread recognition that human behavior is having a destructive and potentially catastrophic effect on our planet, corporations and environmental organizations are capitalizing on the public's increasing willingness to make eco-friendly consumer choices. To this end they are promoting "eco" or "green" labeling to identify for consumers what is produced in accordance with prescribed "sustainability" standards.

At first impression, environmental campaigns such as these appear legitimate because they appeal to something within us that is worthy and good—an inherent sense of compassion that tells us we should care about what happens to our planet and the other species who share it with us, and adjust our choices accordingly. Yet to the extent that some of them stop short of defining or prescribing what is actually required of us to achieve these ideals, these campaigns fail to inspire the expression of true environmental values.

---

*Right now, unfortunately, our laws sometimes mandate that new flavors be tested on animals. Obviously we do not believe that it is ethical to use animals to test these new flavors. In working to ensure product innovation, the animal rights movement needs to work just as hard to ensure that an increase in vegan products based on meat and dairy analogs does not paradoxically result in an increase in animal testing, a factor that animal rights groups can more effectively control if they take a leadership position in their creation. Thankfully, many of these flavors already exist and therefore do not legally require additional testing.

To many environmentalists, animals are judged worthy of activism on their behalf in relation to how useful they are to humans or how many members of their species exist. There is no objection to taking the lives of animals such as crows or rats, species that are plentiful or have no material value to humans. Yet if there are limited numbers of a species, environmentalists advocate that we adjust behaviors negatively impacting their numbers. For instance, some environmental organizations have mounted campaigns encouraging the public to eat only fish caught in accordance with their "sustainability" standards. These organizations are seeking to ensure the continuation of certain fish because some species, those which historically have been exploited as food, are being pushed to the brink of extinction by what they call "overfishing." Ultimately what they want are limitations on how many animals of a certain species can be killed. Killing is acceptable so long as it falls within certain parameters. In other words, they want to make sure we don't kill *all* the fish so that there will be *some* left to kill indefinitely. That is the essence of the environmental philosophy which predominates today, but is this really what "environmentalism" should be?

The ultimate goal of the environmental movement is to create a peaceful and harmonious relationship between humans and the environment. To be authentic, this goal must include respect for animals who are an integral part of that environment. The environmental movement's embrace of "sustainability" as it relates to the killing of animals violates this ideal and tragically perpetuates the harmful idea that we should view animals as *resources*, their value determined by their usefulness to humans or how many there are, rather than as individuals with an intrinsic right to exist. In doing so, it embraces, rather than challenges, the underlying causes of the destruction it claims to oppose, sanctions further destruction by cloaking the killing of some animals in an environment-friendly guise, and promotes the pernicious idea that killing animals is consistent with respect for the planet and its inhabitants.

As such, modern environmentalism has more in common with the industries to blame for environmental problems than its proponents care to admit. And, unlike other social movements, it lacks a coherent and rigorous moral foundation from which its tenets and advocacy are derived. It has yet to evolve into what it should be: a rights-based philosophy, one that seeks unequivocal protection for the earth's non-human inhabitants not only because they have an unalienable right to such but because a truly harmonious relationship with the environment is simply not possible so long as we continue to kill them. Vegans prove that there is a kinder, gentler way for humans to meet their needs, one that does not rely on exploiting and killing our fellow earthlings or the plundering of our planet that comes with it.

the most inconvenient truth of them all

The focus on "sustainability" labeling is misleading on many levels. Companies label meat, eggs, and dairy products as such, even though the taste for these is taking a heavy toll on the planet. Animal agriculture is the leading cause of climate change, accounting for over 50% of greenhouse emissions, more than all other sources combined.

Old Habits Die Easily

When we put meat-eating in an historical context—that is, when we stop to consider that our ancestors ate meat since before we were even fully human—it can be overwhelming to imagine ever changing that habit. In fact, those who defend the right of humans to eat animals will argue that, as a species, we have always eaten animals, and they cite that point to defend the "right" of humans to continue to do so now. But if we buy into the "we've always done it this way" argument, there is no end to the atrocities that we could defend with such sloppy logic. Slavery, sexism, homophobia, racism, and imperialism have dominated most cultures throughout human history until very recently. That such mores and practices defined our ancestors doesn't mean they should continue to define us, especially when we have the awareness and ability to do better.

Had animal products not been available, our ancestors would have experimented with other sources that served the same purpose and end they were seeking.

To fall prey to the defeatist notion that humans will always eat animals and their products because we always have, one must ignore another significant historical fact that makes the goal of widespread veganism feasible: eating habits are changing all the time. The human diet has always been in a state of flux, constantly evolving in response to various factors including migration, famine, weather, technological advances, and, more recently, nutritional awareness. The consumption of meat and other animal products has depended mainly on their availability rather than on a philosophical belief that we should consume the bodies of other living beings. Because chickens were available, our ancestors ate chickens. Because their eggs were available, they learned how to use them for various purposes in recipes. Had animal products not been available, they would have experimented with other sources that served the same purpose and end they were seeking and today those ingredients would be in widespread use instead. The pervasiveness of meat, eggs, and dairy products is an inherited cultural legacy, in the same way their absence in other cultures which do not, for example, eat cows or drink milk, is an historical inheritance and nothing more. Animals are eaten primarily out of habit and convenience, not ideology.

If one human characteristic accounts for our global domination, it is our adaptability. In the time it took humans to migrate from Africa to every part of Earth, our early ancestors and their many generations of offspring traveled through constantly changing landscapes and climates. And so, out of necessity, did their diets, clothing, and housing. Our ability to adapt, to change, is a hallmark of our species.

Simple exposure to alternatives can foster change and erode old habits.

On a small scale you can witness this phenomenon in our family. If you compare the number of vegans to meat-eaters in both of our extended families, the vegans have it by an impressive margin—powerful proof that veganism is contagious. Moreover, a peek at the diets of steadfast meat-eaters in the family, who are surrounded by vegan spouses, sons, daughters, nieces, nephews, grandkids, and in-laws, is just as instructive about how simple exposure to alternatives can foster change and erode old habits.

So far there is only one vegan in the family, Nathan's sister, Rachel, who is "raw," meaning that for health reasons she does not eat food that is heated over 115 degrees. Her diet consists of fresh fruits, vegetables, roots, and nuts that are blended, beaten, smashed, powdered, dehydrated, and otherwise prepared in innovative ways but never cooked. Her devotion to eating the healthiest diet imaginable, and the foods to which she has exposed us, has inspired everyone in our immediate family to eat better. When she comes to visit, we gladly accommodate her needs by accompanying her to local restaurants specializing in raw foods.

There is a rule in our family that whenever we go out to eat it's at either a vegan restaurant or one with plenty of vegan options, and everyone eats vegan. For the most part the outnumbered meat-eaters in the family are good sports about this arrangement. If they grumble, we remind them that their compliance is nothing less than ethics demand, and they smile, suck it up, and eat vegan. The only one who ever has the *chutzpah* to express real discontent is Nathan's father, Izzy. Eighty-nine and hard of hearing, he is often befuddled as to why, exactly, we eat the way we do. "No fish? What's wrong with fish?" he exclaims in astonishment every time we explain that they are "off menu." So it was with great trepidation that we awaited his reaction when he experienced raw food for the first time.

Food at raw restaurants often imitates conventional "foods" such as pizza, hamburgers, or nachos, and they use these labels to describe dishes that sometimes share little in common with the original. Therefore, when we took Izzy out for his first raw dining experience, certain expectations were created when we told him that we had ordered him his favorite food—"bagels and lox." These expectations were dashed when the waiter placed before him an enigmatic, bagel-shaped concoction of seaweed, cashew cheese, red onions, sunflower seeds, and capers. He stared a moment, trying to comprehend that this was the bagel dish we had promised him; then he huffed audibly and pushed the plate across the table.

After this show of obvious displeasure, we encouraged him to give it a try and went on eating our food, feigning disinterest as to what he would do next. Though no one said a word about it, there was a collective understanding that we would give him the space to change his mind. So we all pretended not to notice when he stealthily reached for his plate and began eating, first slowly and tentatively, then quite voraciously. His scowl was replaced by a smile, and five minutes later he ordered a second "bagels and lox."

Now when this kosher, Polish octogenarian comes for a visit, where does he ask to eat? At a raw restaurant run by a hippie cult in Berkeley. "They make lox real nice," he tells us.

Anything is possible.

ANIMAL RIGHTS
AS AMERICAN AS THE FOURTH OF JULY

We hold these truths to be self evident, that all men are created equal. That they are endowed by their creator with certain unalienable rights, that among these are life, liberty and the pursuit of happiness.

AN EVER MORE PERFECT UNION

As much as they have shaped American history, these words in the Declaration of Independence will continue to shape its future. While the Revolutionary War they sparked may be long over, the battles for liberation they inspired are not, as disenfranchised groups build on their foundation to win equal rights and equal protection under the law. By exposing the hypocrisy that one group's rights were regarded as "self evident," while theirs were not acknowledged at all, abolitionists, suffragists, civil rights activists, disabled rights advocates, and others have all invoked the Declaration of Independence in their own quest to realize it's promise and to help us build a more perfect union. But there are still billions of individuals who do not yet have the rights we demand and accept as unalienable for ourselves. Though we may differ in some regards, animals share the things the Declaration proclaims matter most: the desire to live, to be free, and to be happy. In these significant ways, humans and non-human animals are identical. Yet tragically, most Americans make choices every day which imply otherwise, especially when they sit down to eat. Aren't animals entitled to life, liberty, and the pursuit of happiness?

Of course they are.

The American Way

Perhaps more than any other place you are likely to visit, the conventional American grocery store gives you a glimpse of the great melting pot, a slice of Americana. After all, everyone has to eat. In a grocery store you will see people from all walks of life. But one thing you *aren't* likely to see is any of them reading ingredient labels. Because of illness related to obesity, some might look for the phrase "low sodium" or "low fat" if their doctor told them to, but what they won't undertake is an ingredient-by-ingredient review of products. For most Americans, if it is "food" and it tastes "good," that's all they need to know.

One of Jennifer's relatives is a case in point. We would hazard to guess that he has never read an ingredient label in his life. He's no country bumpkin. He holds advanced degrees in engineering and once was the CEO of a Silicon Valley company with Michael Dell and Bill Gates in his Rolodex. Though now retired, he made his living through strategic planning. Like most Americans when it comes to food, however, his policy is no questions asked. He doesn't think about whether something is good for him or not; what the fat, sugar, or sodium content is; whether it is high in cholesterol, natural or artificial, grown in a field or made in a laboratory; what pesticides may have been sprayed on it; or what preservatives may have been added for shelf life. He has just one criterion: taste.

One of his favorite foods is artichoke dip, which he buys at the deli counter of his local grocery store. Even though he knows we are both vegan, he still asks us whether we want to taste it because the name of the food does not indicate an animal product. Quite simply artichoke dip must be vegan because artichokes are a vegetable. Never mind that the first ten ingredients are a combination of milk, butter, cream, sour cream, cheese, whey, and flavorings derived from dairy products. And never mind that artichoke does not make an appearance until the very bottom of the ingredient list. How would he know? He never looked. By the same token he thinks that his favorite brand of steak sauce, which is vegan, is not vegan because it has the word "steak" in its name and is meant to pour on meat. He is a very successful, highly educated, intelligent man who has never bothered to spend much time thinking about his food choices other than how they taste. And, as he will freely admit, he never will.

That is how most Americans eat. They shouldn't. Americans are overweight, unhealthy, and dying prematurely because of it. But simply telling them to increase their fruit and vegetable consumption, reconfiguring the "food" groups, or adding more information to product labels they aren't reading anyway isn't working. These messages have been drilled into us for the last several decades, and our obesity epidemic is only getting worse. So if people aren't going to change and the food can, it should.

Today we can make a vegan version of every food that Americans like. Doing so will not only help save animals but also improve people's health. If we can eliminate the biggest barrier preventing people from giving up the consumption of animals—not wanting to sacrifice "taste"—by giving them the same foods but in a vegan version, why aren't we?

Things We Ignore at Our Own Peril

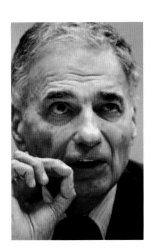

There's No Place Like Home

We love to travel! There are so many wonderful reasons to do so. It is a relaxing way to escape the tedious tasks of everyday life such as doing the dishes, folding the laundry, cleaning the house, or shopping for groceries. More significantly, travel affords the excitement of seeing first-hand things you've only read or heard about: historic landmarks, beautiful natural places, or famous works of art. And experiencing how others live fosters not only a greater understanding of other people but also greater self-awareness. Traveling promotes perspective, not just for new places, but for home as well, by allowing you to appreciate things to which familiarity has made you blind.

Several years ago, while traveling in Australia, we had one such eye-opening experience that made us appreciate how much progress veganism has made in the United States. Our travels coincided with an increasing frustration at our country's failure to address many of its most pressing problems, including unaffordable health care, the increasing divide between rich and poor, the climate crisis, and our nation's crumbling infrastructure. Australians, on the other hand, had already enjoyed universal health care for 35 years and were ranked number four in the world for life expectancy, compared to the States which ranked an abysmal 42nd. And while reports were indicating that the number of Americans slipping into poverty was increasing at an alarming rate, the minimum wage in Australia was double that of the U.S. We were ready to get away and we fully expected our flight to take us not only to another country but also a more progressive reality.

Before leaving, we did all the research necessary to ensure that we'd have places to eat during our stay down

under. Nonetheless, we were surprised to find our options quite limited. One city included a vegan juice bar, a natural food market, and three "vegetarian-friendly" restaurants, of which we were to discover two had already gone out of business. Unfortunately, while the open one was *vegetarian*, it did not offer a single vegan option. With no vegan restaurants to dine at, we fell back on the old stand-by of Indian and Italian restaurants for dinner, enjoying aloo gobi and cheeseless pizza. But it was trying to find a satisfying vegan lunch at the natural food store and juice bar one afternoon that led to an epiphany.

From the outside looking in we knew we were headed for a disappointment. On display in the store window was a tragic assortment of dried beans, burlap bags overflowing with dried beans, and large silver scoops filled with—you guessed it—dried beans. While the display made it abundantly clear that this was *the* place to be if you were a connoisseur of dried beans, it was, on the whole, a display entirely inadequate to its intended purpose of luring the majority of us non-bean aficionados in from the sidewalk.

Inside was little better. Rows and rows and rows of bulk bins, full of grains, nuts and, of course, more dried beans, was pretty much all there was to choose from. The small fridge contained huge buckets of miso and tofu, but other than some dried fruit and energy bars that contained whey and honey, there was nothing—either in or out of the fridge—that could be consumed immediately. And there was certainly nothing our kids, accustomed to vegan analogs of typical American fare, could have been persuaded to eat. It looked, it felt, and, due to a pungent odor of vitamins, it smelled like 20 years ago.

And so it was on to the juice bar a few blocks away, which according to our research sold a little food, a claim we were soon to realize depended, in the spirit of President Clinton, on what your definition of "food" is. This time there was a selection of ready-made items, but again the visuals afforded by the deli case served more as cautionary tale than enticement. One item in particular that stood out was a concoction labeled "sushi," four inches wide and filled not only with brown rice but also with what must have been every scrap of fruit, vegetable, and grain left over from making the other items on display. Wrapped in a thin layer of seaweed were sunflower seeds, alfalfa sprouts, beans, chopped kale, corn, dried papaya chunks, a couple of sultanas (Australian raisins), and something shiny that frighteningly resembled the old boot from Monopoly. We dubbed it "The Great Vegan Cliché Roll." Is it possible that anyone would ever order TGVCR? We were desperate, but not that desperate.

Foregoing the date chunks and powdered flax seed, we ordered banana smoothies from the guy at the counter, the friendliest mate you'd ever want to meet. When we explained that we were from the States, his eyes grew wide, and seeking confirmation of a rumor he had heard, he asked, "Is it true you have giant grocery stores full of organic and vegan food?"

Before answering, we had to think a moment. *Was this a trick question?* We couldn't conceive that full-service grocery stores with organic and vegan food would come as a shock to anyone living in the twenty-first century. But with the dawning realization that apparently it was, we answered, "Yes, as a matter of fact we do!" And we left with a renewed appreciation for what, for so long now, we have taken for granted, almost forgetting how it was in the United States a mere two decades ago. When it comes to vegan options, there is no place like home.

In the United States we already have much of the foundation necessary to promote veganism to a wider audience. We already have many stores that are willing to sell vegan products, and we already have a large number of companies producing tasty vegan foods. The stage is set for a vegan revolution. The lights are on, the curtains are up, and the audience waits in anticipation. Fellow animal activists, let's break a leg!

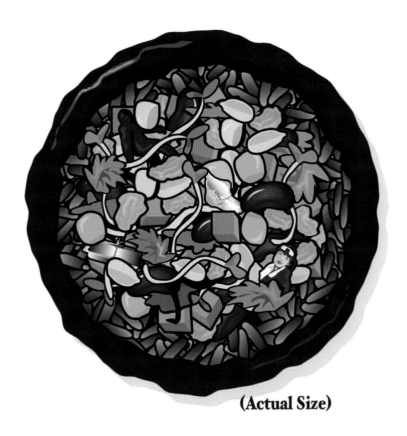

(Actual Size)

The Great Vegan Cliché Roll

To out great surprise, someone did order TGVCR after we sat down to our smoothies. By the time we finished them, planned the rest of our day, and read the local newspaper, he had barely finished swallowing the first bite. We can only imagine how bad his jaw must have hurt the next day from all that chewing.

"What Color is Your Aura?"

Veganism means not eating or using any product that comes from an animal. It's that simple. But you wouldn't know it from appearances. Veganism often comes wrapped in a lot of "health" food and New Age mumbo-jumbo that spooks those to whom we most need to appeal if veganism is ever to be widespread: Middle Americans—a.k.a. soccer moms and NASCAR dads—who already assume that vegans must spend breakfast, lunch, and dinner on their hands and knees grazing on the front lawn.

We certainly don't discourage this caricature with our obsessive focus on the healthful aspects of veganism. Just whom are we trying to convince? With so many Americans suffering from obesity, it is clear that for most Americans, taste trumps health. We must make the taste, and not just the other benefits of a vegan diet compete with the taste of an animal-based one.

Eve may have been tempted with a juicy organic apple, but only because her alternative was a salad. Today's vegan neophyte is more likely to succumb to a Big Mac. We will not prevail by offering apples, or worse, a bulgur wheat and quinoa salad with cucumber raita. In fact, had the Almighty countered temptation by offering Eve "chicken" fried seitan, vegan mashed potatoes with gravy, and vegan chocolate cake for dessert, we'd still be living in paradise. We must balance the terms of engagement. In other words, we need to fight fire with fire.

No more vegan cookbooks with raw vegetables on the cover; no more equating veganism with kamut, spelt, amaranth, or other obscure grains from long-lost civilizations; no more sacrificing the taste and familiarity of veganism by accommodating every damned food allergy there is. And, for goodness sake, let us have no more talk of auras, karma, and spirituality.

Things Vegans Should NEVER Say When Discussing Veganism with Non-Vegans

"Soak overnight"
But we're hungry *now*. In a world full of fast food, we won't win with delayed gratification. *Think microwave.*

"Carob"
Chocolate is vegan. Enough said.

"Spirulina" or "blue-green algae"

What purpose could possibly justify the perilous introduction of the word "algae" into a conversation about veganism?

"Macrobiotic"

After all, no one knows what it means anyway.

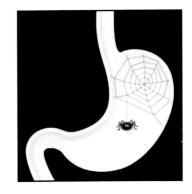

"Fasting"
Oh, so it goes like this: never eat meat, eggs, or dairy products, and some days don't eat at all?

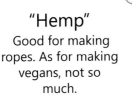

"Hemp"
Good for making ropes. As for making vegans, not so much.

"Gluten-free"

We feel bad for people with food allergies, and would love for them to become vegan, but when and how did the gluten-free crowd hijack veganism? We've already got enough food restrictions as it is, thank you very much.

"Chutney"
American condiments only, please. Pass the ketchup, mustard, hot sauce, mayo, and relish (we'll make exceptions for soy sauce and salsa).

Things Vegans Should NEVER Say When Discussing Veganism with Non-Vegans

"Sprouted foods"

According to health food activists, sprouted beans have the vitamin A content of a lemon, the thiamin of an avocado, the riboflavin of an apple, the niacin of a banana, and the ascorbic acid of a loganberry. But so does a multivitamin, and you can swallow without having to taste it.

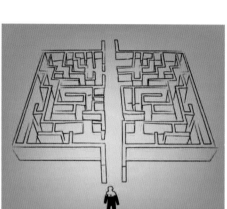

"Amino acids"

Why complicate the uncomplicated?

RIP

"COMPLETE PROTEIN" 1971-1981

Old-school vegetarianism. May it rest in peace.

"Whole grains"

For Americans, processed equals tasty equals appealing.

"Hours of preparation time"

Convenience, convenience, convenience! Jarred, frozen, canned, and other ready-made vegan foods are an animal's best friend.

"Couscous"

A no-no! It serves no purpose that white rice can't serve better.

"Bulgur wheat"

Possibly the two most unappetizing words in the English language.

"Broccoli, kale, and arugula"

The only thing Americans like that is this green has pictures of dead presidents on it and comes in denominations of $1, $5, $10, $20, $50, etc. We'll make an exception for the vegetables that make up the traditional American side salad—iceberg lettuce, a few meager shavings of carrot, and a cherry tomato or two—but only if they come smothered in a creamy dressing.

"Omega-3"
Yawwwwwn. "I'm sorry, did you say something?"

"Wheat grass"
Let's not confirm the suspicion that we actually do eat grass.

"Colon cleansing"

Never talk about your colon or use the word with anyone except your doctor, and even then only with the proper sheepishness, downcast gaze, stammering of voice, and shuffling of feet. And if he or she recommends a colonoscopy, drink heavily afterward to drown your shame and always wear sunglasses when talking to that doctor thereafter. Better yet, change your HMO.

"Spirituality, enlightenment ..."

And other variations of this topic including the soul, the goddess, the light, higher consciousness, awakening, purity, auras, higher planes, universal truths, harmonic convergence, past lives, reincarnation, Zen, chakras, Gaia, karma, kundalini, morphogenetic fields, psychic ability, spiritual healing, astrology, esotericism, metaphysics, alternative medicine, phrases such as "all is one" or "mind-body-spirit," and yes, just to play it safe, even meditation and yoga. Discussion of "tantric sex" is okay, but only if the person you are talking to is a hippie and you are trying to score with said hippie.

A Field Guide to the

Modern American Vegan Family

Vegan spotting! As the number of vegans nationwide continues to grow, this fun hobby is easier today than ever before. So take out those binoculars and see how many you can find. Following is a field guide with some helpful hints that will make spotting a wide variety of vegans quick and simple!

Identifying Characteristics

Vegans come in all colors, sizes, and ages. This can sometimes make identifying vegans difficult. That is why paying close attention to other distinguishing characteristics is so important. For vegans, food is just the beginning. Being vegan is a way of life, so clothing, accessories, and habitat can also be helpful in identification. But look closely! Vegans are known for their uncanny ability to blend in with their surroundings by mimicking traditional American habits but in animal-friendly versions.

Lunch box filled with tasty vegan treats

Clothing free of leather, fur, wool, or silk

Synthetic sports equipment

FEMALE CHILD

MALE CHILD

Where to Look

Knowing where to look for vegans is just as important as knowing what to look for. You are unlikely to spot vegans in the meat section of the grocery store, or at zoos, aquariums, and other places where animals are held in captivity. Vegan hot spots include vegetarian restaurants and natural food stores.

Homo Sapien Sapien Vegania Americanus

ADULT FEMALE

COMPANION ANIMAL

ADULT MALE

NATURAL HABITAT

How many vegans can you spot?

*The term "cruelty-free" means that a product was not tested on animals. However, some cruelty-free products are not vegan so it is important to check that they are also labeled as having no animal-derived ingredients.

Shocking Upset!
Broccoli-Based Restaurant Chain "McHealthy" Fails to Make Top 100

What do Americans typically eat? A look at the top-grossing restaurants provides the answer. Restaurants that serve healthy foods rich in flax seed oil, whole grains popular with the Aztecs, and cruciferous vegetable-based dishes do not appear anywhere on the list, which covered the top 400. Here's the top ten of the list, which repeats different versions of the same standard fare over and over again:

1. **McDonald's**
2. **KFC**
3. **Burger King**
4. **Subway**
5. **Pizza Hut**
6. **Wendy's**
7. **Taco Bell**
8. **Domino's Pizza**
9. **Dunkin' Donuts**
10. **Applebee's**

For many reasons this list should inspire horror. These restaurants serve food that is cruel to animals, destructive to the planet, and high in fat, sodium, and cholesterol. But there is another lesson animal activists should heed from this information: our fellow Americans aren't very picky, are they? We're not dealing with palates refined on artisan cheeses and aged meats. In fact, to a "foodie," there isn't even any "food" for sale at the restaurants that Americans frequent, a fact which can work to the animals' advantage. Switch the meat and cheese in a McDonald's Quarter-Pounder with vegan versions that look and taste identical, and no one will notice. Likewise in a Taco Bell Burrito Supreme. Most Americans have no idea what their food is really made of, nor do they care, so long as their food is familiar and tastes good. If it looks like cheese, if it tastes like cheese, if it is called cheese, by golly, it is cheese!

We believe that the most important choice each of us can make to help animals is to become vegan. But our advice to those who want to do more, who want to have an impact beyond their own humane choices, and who want to help pave the way for a vegan society, is that you don't need to work or volunteer for large animal rights organizations to do so. In our more than forty years of combined activism, we've met a lot of people working on their own and getting great results. They've saved the lives of companion animals and wild animals, as well as animals used for "entertainment," animals raised for "food," and animals in laboratories. They've succeeded in defeating harmful legislation, and they've succeeded in passing pro-animal legislation. And they did this against powerful industry opposition, often without the support of the large national organizations. You can make a difference, too.

From urging owners of local restaurants and grocery stores to expand vegan options, to teaching classes on vegan substitution, to ensuring that local natural food stores and traditional grocery stores stock the latest and greatest vegan products, there is a lot one person can do to convert more people to veganism and bring it into the mainstream. Big changes can come from small efforts, and new activists will be amazed at what they can accomplish once they grant themselves the authority to try. Visit allamericanvegan.com for ideas and materials for effective vegan activism.

Psst - Hey You, Animal Lover. Come Over Here.

Before You Go, We Need to Talk to You for a Minute

Okay, admittedly we digress, but opportunities like this don't come along every day, so let us bend your ear for a moment. Since you are reading a vegan cookbook, we figure that there is a good chance you love animals. If you do, we thought you might want to know about something tragic that is happening in the animal protection movement right now, something you have the power to help make right.

We both became animal rights activists after working in animal rescue involving dogs and cats. It was, in fact, such work that opened our hearts and minds to concern for all animals, regardless of species. And so you can imagine our surprise when we discovered that within the animal rights movement itself, there is a double standard regarding companion animals. While most animal rights organizations boldly proclaim that we should not kill animals for any reason, they make an exception when it comes to the millions of animals in our nation's pounds and "shelters." This killing, they argue, is humane and necessary and, as the leader of the nation's largest "animal rights" group once proclaimed, "a gift"—*even in the face of readily available lifesaving alternatives.*

Time and time again those working to promote the rights of dogs and cats have found that the national animal rights organizations not only fail to support them but also misrepresent, malign, and even fiercely condemn them. Why? Because when it comes to the killing of dogs and cats, it is mostly the animal protection movement itself that is doing the killing at the roughly 3,500 "shelters" in the U.S. In addition, not only have some animal rights leaders worked at these same animal "shelters," but they also have done a lot of killing—and some still do.

For over a century animal "shelters" in this country have argued that the killing of animals is unavoidable and that the "irresponsible" American public is to blame. Without an alternative model to challenge the assumptions upon which these calculations were based, animal "shelters" by default were granted a license to kill millions of animals a year while blaming others for the need to do so. Not only did this stymie any innovation to end the killing, but it had the unfortunate side effect of creating a mindset among shelter directors who, having gone unchallenged for so long, expect that they should be able to operate without public scrutiny, comment, or accountability for their actions and decisions.

By the early 2000s, when the burgeoning No Kill movement proved that the assumptions upon which traditional sheltering was based were untrue and that animals entering "shelters" could be saved, conventional models based on killing had become so firmly entrenched that any challenge was met with recrimination and hostility. Since that time No Kill advocates throughout the country have found themselves at cross-purposes not only with their local "shelters" but just as often with national animal protection groups that defend these "shelters" and their archaic, regressive policies which favor killing.

As a result, it is not uncommon for "shelters" to refuse the assistance of grassroots rescue organizations willing to save the animals they are determined to kill. All across the country, "shelters" are holding animals hostage, ignoring the requests of local No Kill sanctuaries and non-profit rescue groups willing to assume responsibility for their care, even as they turn around and kill them. For far too long those running our nation's animal "shelters," agencies funded by the philanthropic donations and tax dollars of an animal-loving American public, have refused to alter the way they operate, stop the killing that is within their power to end, and mirror the progressive values about dogs and cats that most Americans hold dear.

Sadly, the movement to end the killing of dogs and cats in animal "shelters" is too animal rights for many of those in the animal rights movement because it requires challenging the animal rights powers-that-be. In fact, far from being leaders when it comes to championing the rights of dogs and cats who enter animal "shelters," the animal rights movement is, tragically, the No Kill movement's most vociferous opponent, with just a few organizations being rare and notable exceptions. Right now, the average American is far more progressive and humane when it comes to dogs and cats than the largest animal protection groups in the nation.

The animal rights movement's support of killing is not only a deadly betrayal of dogs, cats, and the other animals entering "shelters," it undermines their stated goals for all animals. It is the public's love and compassion for companion animals that could support laws banning killing in animal "shelters" altogether *right now*. The legally guaranteed right to life for a species of non-human animal will be a crossing of the Rubicon from which our society will never return. History and the human rights movement predict that the door, once opened, will, with time, be pushed open ever wider to accommodate other species of animals currently being exploited or killed in other contexts. Right now, however, the nation's largest animal rights groups are working to ensure that that door remains firmly shut.

So please be careful which groups you support in the hope of promoting the rights and welfare of animals. Tragically, things aren't what they seem or should be in the animal rights movement. Dig a little deeper, arm yourself with the facts, and demand better. Please help us reform the animal rights movement and bring dogs and cats into its protective embrace. They need our voice too. Visit allamericanvegan.com for more information.

Animals in "Shelters" Need YOU

A Word to Our Fellow Animal Activists

We became vegan for ethical reasons, and we believe other people should do the same. The purpose of this book is not to offer an excuse or absolution for people who eat animals, which results in brutal suffering and killing, but to explain it in a way that illuminates what can be done to stop the practice. We have chosen to focus on the potential for widespread veganism that we believe already exists. And we trust that our fellow animal rights activists will not misconstrue our intent or doubt our dedication to animal liberation.

About the Authors

Nathan

Nathan is a graduate of Stanford Law School and a former criminal prosecutor as well as corporate attorney. A vegan for over 20 years, he has helped write animal protection legislation, spoken internationally on animal issues, created successful No Kill programs, and has consulted with animal protection groups all over the world. Under his leadership, Tompkins County, New York, became the first No Kill community in the United States. Nathan is the author of two books: *Redemption: The Myth of Pet Overpopulation and the No Kill Revolution in America*, which won five national awards; and *Irreconcilable Differences: The Battle for the Heart and Soul of America's Animal Shelters*. Nathan is the national director of the No Kill Advocacy Center, a non-profit organization dedicated to ending the systematic killing of animals in U.S. shelters.

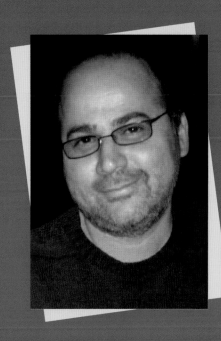

Jennifer

Jennifer has been vegan and worked in the animal rights movement for over 20 years. She has written guides to vegan living and taught vegan cooking classes. She is a founding Board Member of the No Kill Advocacy Center and currently divides her time between promoting the No Kill philosophy, vegan cooking, and homeschooling her children. This is her first book.

The Winograds live in the San Francisco Bay Area with their two children and a menagerie of animal companions.

INDEX

Note: Recipes and their page numbers are highlighted in red.